Keep Your Spiritual Edge

Keep Your Spiritual Edge

Lessons from Andrew Bonar for Ministers Today

David P. Beaty

Reformation Heritage Books
Grand Rapids, Michigan

Reformation Heritage Books
3070 29th St. SE
Grand Rapids, MI 49512
616-977-0889
orders@heritagebooks.org
www.heritagebooks.org

Scripture taken from the New King James Version®. Copyright © 1982 by Thomas Nelson. Used by permission. All rights reserved.

Printed in the United States of America
23 24 25 26 27 28/10 9 8 7 6 5 4 3 2 1

Library of Congress Cataloging-in-Publication Data

Names: Beaty, David P., author.
Title: Keep your spiritual edge : lessons from Andrew Bonar for
    ministers today / David P. Beaty.
Description: Grand Rapids, Michigan : Reformation Heritage Books,
    [2023] | Includes bibliographical references.
Identifiers: LCCN 2022041166 (print) | LCCN 2022041167 (ebook)
    | ISBN 9781601789969 (paperback) | ISBN 9781601789976
    (epub)
Subjects: LCSH: Clergy—Religious life. | Bonar, Andrew A. (Andrew
    Alexander), 1810-1892.
Classification: LCC BV4011.6 .B42 2023 (print) | LCC BV4011.6
    (ebook) | DDC 248.8/92—dc23/eng/20221107
LC record available at https://lccn.loc.gov/2022041166
LC ebook record available at https://lccn.loc.gov/2022041167

For additional Reformed literature, request a free book list from Reformation Heritage Books at the above regular or email address.

Contents

Introduction

I don't know of a better model of humble servanthood, pastoral faithfulness, biblical scholarship, zealous evangelism, and growing love for God throughout a long ministry than Andrew A. Bonar. The Scottish pastor who died in 1892 is not well known today. He is sometimes remembered as the brother of hymn writer Horatius Bonar. He is more often mentioned as the biographer of his good friend, Robert Murray M'Cheyne (1813–1843). Titled *The Memoir and Remains of Robert Murray M'Cheyne*, Bonar's biography and compilation of M'Cheyne's work became a bestseller after its publication in 1844 and is still in print. M'Cheyne's name became synonymous with holiness, prayer, and deep spirituality. Had Andrew Bonar not written about Robert M'Cheyne, few would have heard of the young Scottish pastor and his remarkable walk with God.

But Bonar's life was equally remarkable—and in some ways, even more so. The close communion with God that was so characteristic of M'Cheyne during his seven years as a pastor was seen throughout Andrew Bonar's fifty-five years in ministry. M'Cheyne never married, and his singleness afforded him time to seek and serve the Lord "without distraction" (1 Cor. 7:35). Bonar was married and faced the challenges of raising a family while serving a large church. While M'Cheyne suffered with physical infirmity throughout adulthood, Bonar's sufferings were of a different type. He experienced both the loss of a child and the loss of his wife while he served as a pastor. M'Cheyne was called as pastor to St. Peter's Church, a congregation of one thousand in Dundee, Scotland, where he served until his death. In 1856, Bonar started a new church in Finnieston, near Glasgow, and the church had grown to one thousand by the time of his death in 1892. M'Cheyne's years at St. Peter's were marked by a powerful outpouring of the Holy Spirit. The work of the Spirit during Bonar's years at Finnieston was less dramatic and received less attention but also resulted in hundreds of conversions and steady growth of the church.

Robert Murray M'Cheyne's life shows us what God can do through a devoted servant during a few short years on earth. Andrew Bonar's life shows us what He can do through decades of faithful service.

Those who knew Andrew Bonar testified of the observable evidence of God's Spirit at work in his life. Shortly after Bonar's death, a number of tributes were written by friends and acquaintances. Theodore Cuyler wrote, "A more sweet-spirited man I never knew." Comparing Bonar with other "noble men" in the Free Church of Scotland, Cuyler also wrote that there were "none who combined sweetness and strength in a more loveable and holy union than Andrew A. Bonar."[1] Rev. Alex Rattray recalled Andrew Bonar's humility as "one of those characteristics of Dr. Bonar that made everybody love him." Further describing his modesty, Rattray wrote, "If you were not carried away by the man's teaching, which was likely as not, yet were you infallibly carried away by the man himself—the meek and gracious spirit that softened and beautified everything it touched."[2]

Another friend lamented Bonar's death by writing, "He was a man of saintly character, and of a bright and happy disposition. His name, wherever it was known, was surrounded with a halo of sanctity."[3]

The best source for learning about Bonar's life is *The Diary and Life of Andrew A. Bonar*, edited by Marjory Bonar and published by the Banner of Truth Trust. This book combines diary entries and letters with Marjory Bonar's *Reminiscences of His Life* and provides an excellent overview of Andrew Bonar's life and ministry. My purpose in writing this book is not to attempt another biography but rather to seek to learn from Bonar's remarkable walk with God. I have drawn from *The Diary and Life* but have also made use of Bonar's books and tracts. He wrote several books, introductions to other books, and dozens of tracts. These materials provide rich insights into his ever-increasing love for God and His people.

---

1. Fergus Ferguson, *Rev. A. A. Bonar. D. D.* (Glasgow: John J. Rae, 1893), 160, 173.

2. Ferguson, *Bonar*, 193.

3. Ferguson, *Bonar*, 198–99.

One of the most notable things about Andrew Bonar is that he was so ordinary. He was not an exceptionally gifted preacher, visionary, or leader. Yet the closeness of his walk with God was extraordinary, and it seemed to grow throughout his life. The zeal that marked the start of Andrew Bonar's ministry increased throughout his long pastorate, and he seems to have been purposeful about that. His daughter wrote,

> Dr. Bonar used to tell, with great solemnity, what was said to him at the beginning of his ministry by an old friend and minister: "Remember it is a remark of old and experienced men, that very few men, and very few *ministers*, keep up to the end the edge that was on their spirit at the first."[4]

Andrew Bonar serves as an example of one of the "very few."

---

4. Marjory Bonar, ed., *The Diary and Life of Andrew A. Bonar* (Edinburgh: Banner of Truth, 2013), 252.

Chapter 1

The Life and Ministry of Andrew Bonar

Andrew Bonar was born in Edinburgh in 1810 to James and Marjory Bonar, godly parents who continued the Christian spiritual heritage of several generations of Bonars. Andrew was only eleven when his father died, and the family was cared for by his mother and his oldest brother James. Two of Andrew's older brothers, John and Horatius, became well-known ministers.

Despite the godly influence of his family, Andrew indicates that it was not until age twenty that he received assurance of salvation. In a diary entry dated November 7, 1830, he wrote, "For about two weeks past, ever since I read a passage in Guthrie's *Saving Interest*, I have had a secret joyful hope that I really have believed on the Lord Jesus.... I think that next Communion I may go forward to the Lord's table as one that has received Him."[1]

In 1831 Andrew began theological studies at the Divinity Hall of the University of Edinburgh. He excelled as a student, his expertise in Latin giving support to his great ability with the biblical languages of Greek and

---

1. M. Bonar, *Diary and Life*, 7.

Hebrew. While a student at the Divinity Hall, his life was shaped by the influence of the great Scottish theologian Thomas Chalmers. He was also influenced by his friendship with a group of fellow students. This special band of believers included Alexander Somerville, Alex Moody-Stuart, and Robert Murray M'Cheyne. The group met for prayer every Saturday afternoon in Dr. Chalmers's "vestry." Several also met at 6:30 a.m. on Saturday to study biblical languages.

After completion of his studies, Andrew served probationary periods in two churches, then became pastor at Collace, a county parish in Perthshire. He continued his friendship with Robert M'Cheyne, who served at St. Peter's Church in Dundee, about twenty miles from Collace.

In 1839, the two friends undertook a journey that would shape each of their lives. The Church of Scotland had concern for mission work among the Jewish people and appointed a "Mission of Inquiry" to collect information about the Jews. Bonar and M'Cheyne were asked to join Dr. Alexander Keith and Dr. Alexander Black, two older and more seasoned ministers, on the trip. While both young pastors were reluctant to leave their churches for the six-month mission to the Holy Land, God seemed to confirm His will by the support of their congregations.

The team of four sailed from England in April 1839 to begin the arduous journey that included travel on camelback through deserts in extreme temperatures. The two older men were forced to abandon the trip in Beirut due to health problems, leaving the two young pastors to continue alone.

Bonar and M'Cheyne continued together, facing quarantine due to plague, attack from robbers, and persecution from government and religious authorities. Through it all, they gave out thousands of tracts and shared the gospel with many.

Their research on Jews in France, Italy, Hungary, and Palestine proved to be of much value to the Church of Scotland. In 1841, the first Church of Scotland missionary was sent out to the Jews in Hungary. The record of the mission trip by Bonar and M'Cheyne was published as the *Narrative of a Mission of Inquiry to the Jews from the Church of Scotland* in 1839. By 1847, twenty-three thousand copies were in print, and awareness of the need for missions work among the Jews was increased in Scotland and beyond.

Upon returning home in November 1839, Bonar and M'Cheyne read brief references in a newspaper of a remarkable outpouring of the Holy Spirit in Scotland. Their notes read,

> We were, however, filled with joy, by hearing that God had poured out his Spirit as in the days of old, and we felt it a special kindness to ourselves that the glad tidings should meet us when we were almost in sight of our native land. It appeared also worthy of special notice and thanksgiving that God had done this in the very years that the Church of Scotland had stretched out her hand to seek the welfare of Israel and to speak peace to all their seed.[2]

It was learned that St. Peter's Church had experienced

2. Andrew Bonar and Robert M. M'Cheyne, *Mission of Discovery* (Geanies House: Christian Focus Publications, 1996), 443–44.

a special work of the Spirit through the preaching of William C. Burns, who was serving in M'Cheyne's absence. The revival continued at St. Peter's after M'Cheyne's return and spread to other parts of Scotland.

While Andrew Bonar celebrated the Lord's work at Dundee and elsewhere, he did not see the same reviving work in his own church. His diary entries in the following months indicate his admiration of M'Cheyne and Burns along with his disappointment in his own prayer life and degree of holiness and devotion. On February 3, 1840, he wrote, "The lesson God is teaching me is this, that William Burns is used as the instrument where others have been laboring in vain, because he is much in prayer, beyond all of us."[3] His diary entry for May 29 reads, "I cannot tell how much the thought has struck me of my low attainments at this part of my life, compared with what others have gained. I feel altogether sinful, worthless, something very small and insignificant."[4] And on September 19 he wrote, "I feel my unholiness, my prayerlessness, and much want of solemnity and sense of responsibility. I seem to have done nothing at all for this people.... I feel also a great deal of envy at hearing of others' success."[5]

The humility indicated in Andrew Bonar's diary entries continued throughout his life. He never seemed to feel he was as effective in ministry as some of his friends. But his humility fueled the awareness of his need for God's

---

3. M. Bonar, *Diary and Life*, 37.
4. M. Bonar, *Diary and Life*, 59.
5. M. Bonar, *Diary and Life*, 60.

strength and power. This, he learned, was to be obtained by communion with God in prayer. On January 22, 1841, he wrote, "I have been conversing much with men, and been much outwardly engaged, but I have not been closely, or for any length of time, with God himself. I see, too, that to be close with God gives abundant strength."[6]

While Andrew Bonar grew in deeper communion with God throughout his long life, his friendship with Robert M. M'Cheyne soon came to an end. On May 25, 1843, M'Cheyne died at the age of twenty-nine. Bonar's diary entry for that day reads, "This afternoon about five o'clock, a message has just come to tell me of Robert M'Cheyne's death. Never, never yet in all my life have I felt anything like this: It is a blow to myself, to his people, to the church of Christ in Scotland."[7]

Bonar continued to be affected by his friend's life in the years to come. He seemed to see M'Cheyne as an example of devotion to which he should aspire. Twenty-five years after M'Cheyne's death, he wrote, "It was this day thirty years ago that I was ordained to the ministry. What a long time I have been allowed to work! But the retrospect humbles me to the dust. What would not Robert M'Cheyne have accomplished in so long a time!"[8]

Shortly after M'Cheyne's death in 1843, Andrew Bonar joined over four hundred other ministers in severing their relationship with the Church of Scotland to form

6. M. Bonar, *Diary and Life*, 62.
7. M. Bonar, *Diary and Life*, 69.
8. M. Bonar, *Diary and Life*, 198.

the Free Church of Scotland. Led by Thomas Chalmers and others, these ministers forsook their financial security in the established church in protest of patronage—the appointment of ministers to a local church by nobility or government officials, often without regard to spiritual qualifications. Bonar's daughter wrote of this time, "The effects of this event upon our father's work in Collace were in all respects for the better. He was left free to work as he chose among his people, and even during the trying time when they were without a church in which to worship, God's presence was felt among them, quickening and blessing."[9]

Later in 1843, Bonar began work on *The Memoir and Remains of Robert Murray M'Cheyne*. Remarkably, he finished it by year's end, and it was published in 1844. Within twenty-five years, *The Memoir* had gone through 116 editions. By 1910, an estimated five hundred thousand copies were in print in a number of languages. *The Memoir* became Bonar's best-known book.

While serving at Collace, Bonar also wrote his *Commentary on the Book of Leviticus*, using his knowledge of Hebrew to teach others how the Old Testament sacrifices pointed to Jesus Christ.[10] His next major work was *Redemption Drawing Nigh*, a book that explained his premillennial

9. Marjory Bonar, introduction to *The Good Pastor* (Belfast: Ambassador Publications, 1999).

10. Andrew A. Bonar, *A Commentary on Leviticus* (Edinburgh: Banner of Truth, 1998).

views regarding the second coming of Christ.[11] Throughout his ministry, Bonar wrote a number of tracts and
booklets. Several of these were written for children. *The
True Heaven and the Way to It* is a short, illustrated tract to
help guide children to faith in Jesus. *Gamaliel: A Word to
Young Men* exhorts young men to faithfully follow Christ
throughout their lives and to "beware of neutrality in mat-
ters affecting the soul."[12] His book *Palestine for the Young*
shares knowledge of the Holy Land with young readers.[13]

Bonar also used his talent for research and writing to
bring to light little-known people and stories to inspire
others to deeper devotion to Christ. *Emilia Geddie: A
Child of the Covenant*, about a sixteen-year-old who died in
1681, was written as "an example alike to young and old."[14]
The Monk of Inchcolm was written about a hermit on the
small island of Inchcolm who became a devout follower of
Jesus.[15] *The Martyrs by the Sea* is about two women during
the time of the Covenanters who endured persecution as
"an example of calm faith in confessing Christ's name and
cause."[16] Bonar's tracts and books show him to have been

---

11. Andrew A. Bonar, *Redemption Drawing Nigh* (London: J. Nisbet
& Co., 1847).

12. Andrew A. Bonar, *The True Heaven and the Way to It* and *Gamaliel:
A Word to Young Men*, in *Bonar Collection*.

13. Andrew A. Bonar, *Palestine for the Young* (London: Religious
Tract Society, n.d.).

14. Andrew A. Bonar, *Emilia Geddie: A Child of the Covenant Who
Died in 1681*, in *Bonar Collection*.

15. Andrew A. Bonar, *The Monk of Inchcolm*, in *Bonar Collection*.

16. Andrew A. Bonar, *The Martyrs by the Sea: The Story of the Wigtown
Sufferers*, in *Bonar Collection*.

a disciplined researcher and creative author who always sought to encourage people to more faithful devotion to Jesus Christ.

While pastoring in Collace, Andrew Bonar married his beloved wife, Isabella. She became a loving counselor and faithful colaborer, and the two were blessed with five children. Andrew's daughter Marjory wrote that "his marriage in 1848 increased his usefulness as a pastor, and brought to him new and deeper experiences of life."[17]

After eighteen years in the country pastorate at Collace, Andrew Bonar accepted a call to Glasgow, where he began serving a small group of people at the Finnieston Church. It was difficult to leave the people he loved at Collace, but his conviction was so strong that he told them, "If I did not go to Glasgow I feared I should be acting the part of Jonah." He began his ministry in Glasgow with a great desire for the power of the Holy Spirit. He wrote, "Unless I go forth among them, filled with the Holy Spirit, I see that all will be in vain," and, "It must be a power like that which drew out the people to hear the Baptist in the desert that will draw out the people from these homes. Let me pray much for this."[18]

Though initial progress at Finnieston seemed slow, people began to be drawn to the new pastor and his ability to recognize people and remember their names. In the words of his daughter, "He was everybody's friend. Little children would run up to him as he walked down Fin-

17. M. Bonar, introduction to *The Good Pastor*.
18. M. Bonar, *Diary and Life*, 131.

nieston Street or Grace Street and put their hands in his, looking up to see the loving smile that always greeted them, and to feel the kindly hand laid on their head."[19]

Bonar seemed especially aware of his need to pray more in his new pastorate. In February 1857 he wrote that he was "enabled, after considerable difficulty, to give about four hours this afternoon to waiting upon the Lord in prayer for help and blessing to others as well as to myself."[20]

In April he wrote, "For nearly ten days past have been much divided in prayer, and feel my strength weakened thereby. I must at once return through the Lord's strength to not less than three hours a day spent in prayer and meditation upon the Word."[21]

God honored His servant, and the church at Finnieston grew. There was much evidence of the Spirit's work, and the congregation began to imitate their pastor as people of prayer. But the seasons of joy were broken by sorrow and immense personal loss for Bonar. His young son, Andrew, became seriously ill and died on April 1, 1860. In the depths of grief, Bonar sought more of God's presence. He wrote, "This is the day of our dear little boy's funeral. I do feel today that I love my Lord more than ever, even for what of His ways I see, and the gracious love I can discover already in them."[22]

19. M. Bonar, *Diary and Life*, 134.
20. M. Bonar, *Diary and Life*, 135.
21. M. Bonar, *Diary and Life*, 136.
22. M. Bonar, *Diary and Life*, 149.

Several weeks later he wrote, "I want to live in the love of God, for God, enjoying God, glorifying God, and every day able to tell what new discovery I have made in the fullness of Christ."[23]

Four years later, grief would strike again with the death of his wife, Isabella, just weeks after the birth of their daughter Mary Elizabeth. On October 15, Bonar wrote, "Last night most suddenly, after three hours of sinking, my dear, dear Isabella was taken from me. Lord, pour in comfort, for I cannot. It needs the Holy Ghost to work at such a time."[24]

Bonar's grief continued to turn him to the love and comfort of the Lord: "It is because He is so very great that He can and does attend to each one's smallest care and sorrow. Each one soul is to Him as much as a world, and He can bend down with the same love and loftiness of sympathy on that one as if that one were all."[25]

Despite the seasons of grief he faced, Bonar continued to seek more of God's presence and power in his ministry. The discipline of fasting is mentioned frequently in his diary as he sought to seek God for revival in Glasgow. In 1865 he wrote of a revival in Hillhead and noted, "I have sought the Lord today, by fasting and prayer, that the blessing may come to my people in town also."[26] Bonar believed that prayer and fasting were like the "seed of

---

23. M. Bonar, *Diary and Life*, 150.
24. M. Bonar, *Diary and Life*, 168.
25. M. Bonar, *Diary and Life*, 173.
26. M. Bonar, *Diary and Life*, 177.

blessing to come" and that God would use these to bring about a spiritual harvest.[27]

Bonar felt that his prayer was as important for his church as his preaching. As he prepared to speak as a guest at another church, he wrote, "One of my chief reasons for agreeing to preach tomorrow out of my own pulpit was that I might get this day for prayer, and so might help my people far more than by ordinary preaching."[28]

Especially since the revival associated with W. C. Burns and M'Cheyne in 1839, Andrew Bonar had sought revival and supported evangelistic efforts wherever he saw God's Spirit at work. His own church experienced a significant work of the Holy Spirit in 1874, when he noted that more than seventy people had been converted there.

When American evangelist D. L. Moody visited Scotland, Andrew Bonar took special interest. While many fellow ministers were reluctant to support Moody, Bonar saw his coming as part of God's work in bringing revival to Scotland and went out of his way to support the younger man whose preaching drew huge crowds. Moody and he became friends, and in 1881 at seventy-one years of age, Bonar traveled to America to be a guest at Moody's Northfield Conference.

The latter years of Andrew Bonar's life were filled with preaching, pastoring, writing, and prayer. He was determined never to decrease in his love for communion with God and ministry to God's people. In fact, it seems

27. M. Bonar, *Diary and Life*, 183.
28. M. Bonar, *Diary and Life*, 201.

evident that Bonar's communion with the Lord grew richer as he grew older. In her preface to his *Diary and Life*, his daughter wrote that the book gives "the revelation of the life of one who prayed always, who prayed everywhere, who, the nearer he came to the other world, was every day more constantly enjoying intercourse with it."[29] Until his death at age eighty-two, Andrew Bonar was determined to keep his "spiritual edge."

---

29. M. Bonar, preface to *Diary and Life*.

———— ❧•❧ ————

Chapter 2

Bonar's Preaching and Teaching

Andrew Bonar's ever-increasing love for the Lord was grounded in his ever-deepening love for Scripture and the gospel of grace it reveals. Bonar had embraced the beautiful message of salvation by God's grace through faith in Jesus Christ when he was twenty years old. But a life of Scripture study brought him growing joy in the gospel. His spiritual edge was kept sharp by a lifetime of study. Bonar used his ability with Hebrew and Greek to dig deeply into Scripture, and he delighted in the discoveries of Jesus in both Old and New Testaments. His commentary on the book of Leviticus explains his understanding of how the Old Testament sacrifices point to Christ. Concerning the book of Leviticus, he wrote,

> It will be found that it contains a full system of truth, exhibiting sin and the sinner, grace and the Saviour, comprehending, also, details of duty, and openings into the ages to come—whatever, in short, bears upon a sinner's walk with a reconciled God, and his conversation in this present evil world. Our heavenly Father has

condescended to teach His children by most expressive pictures; and, even in this, much of His love appears.[1]

In the closing words of his *Commentary on Leviticus* (a lengthy volume of 511 pages in its currently published form), Bonar noted that greater joy in the gospel can be realized when one comprehends its presence in the Old Testament: "It is as if the delights of the imagination were superadded to the delights of piety, when the doctrines of the New are expressed in the drapery of the Old economy."[2] Bonar then commended study of the Old Testament to find greater joy in God's grace as we age: "And if there be any aged Christian who has leisure to pursue the employment, we promise him not a different, but the same gospel, seen through a veil of ever-brightening transparency and heightened by time and youthful remembrances."[3]

The reward for digging deeply into those parts of the Bible that seem more difficult to understand can be a richer relationship with Christ. We are reminded of the riches stored for us in the Old Testament when we read the postresurrection account of Jesus's teaching on the road to Emmaus: "And beginning at Moses and all the Prophets, He expounded to them in all the Scriptures the things concerning Himself" (Luke 24:27).

Bonar's only other commentary is also on an Old Testament book. *Christ and His Church in the Book of Psalms* presents Jesus and His work on the cross as central to the

---

1. A. A. Bonar, *Leviticus*, 7–8.

2. A. A. Bonar, *Leviticus*, 511.

3. A. A. Bonar, *Leviticus*, 511.

Psalms. Though the Psalms were written hundreds of years before Christ, Bonar believed that every psalm pointed to some truth related to Jesus. He reminded his readers of the approach of the early Christian church to the Psalms: "Now, in the early ages, men full of the thoughts of Christ could never read the Psalms without being reminded of their Lord."[4] He quoted Augustine, saying that "the voice of Christ and his Church was well-nigh the only voice to be heard in the Psalms."[5]

This was Bonar's approach to the Psalms and, in fact, to all of Scripture. This understanding led him to diligently study all parts of the Bible in order to know Christ better and love Him more. He was a lifelong learner who never tired of new discoveries of the gospel of Jesus Christ through Scripture.

Growing Zeal for Evangelism

Andrew Bonar's love for the gospel fueled his love for sharing it with others. Whether preaching from the Old or New Testament, and seemingly on any passage or topic, Bonar could present the gospel of grace. He knew that preachers were apt to lose sight of this message among other emphases, so he urged church members to pray for their pastors: "Brethren, pray for your pastor, that he may never, to the day of his death, preach a single sermon, or

---

4. Andrew A. Bonar, *Christ and His Church in the Book of Psalms* (Stoke-on-Trent: Tentmaker Publications, 2012), ix.

5. A. A. Bonar, *Christ and His Church*, ix.

be with you in any gathering in His name, without pointing you to the blood shed for the remission of your sin."[6]

It was Bonar's belief that not only pastors but all Christians should be compelled to share the gospel with others. The greater our understanding of the beauty of the gospel, the more our zeal for sharing it with others should overflow. Bonar wrote, "Sit not down in selfish enjoyment when your hearts are burning within you after some fresh discovery of the riches of grace in John 3:16…. Go and tell men these same tidings. And if more were needed to induce you to do so, this might be added, *viz.*, in the very act of telling your fellow men of this salvation you yourself get immense gain."[7]

It was Andrew Bonar's view that sharing the gospel with another person was one of the highest privileges a Christian could ever experience. In his tract *Angel Workers*, he teaches readers what angels might say if given direct messages from God to the church of his day. He envisions what the angel Gabriel might say to his own church: "O tell your *Elders*, and all among your flock who try to proclaim the love of God in sending his Son, that to us their privilege seems the highest that a creature can enjoy. To have such news to proclaim! It passes knowledge!"[8] In a sermon on the work of the Holy Spirit, Bonar said,

---

6. Andrew A. Bonar, *Sheaves after Harvest* (London: Pickering and Inglis, n.d.), 120.

7. A. A. Bonar, *Sheaves*, 123.

8. Andrew A. Bonar, *Gospel Basics* (Edinburgh: Banner of Truth, 2011), 117.

This is a very solemn truth for the Church of God. And at the same time it is a wonderful privilege that is involved in this truth. We are honored to do what angels are not; saints are they who are sent in the footsteps of the Son of Man to seek and save the lost. Angels can only say (almost with envy), "Go you, stand in the temple, and preach all the words of this life" (Acts 5:20); they themselves are not employed on this high errand.[9]

Bonar saw no contradiction between his wholehearted embrace of the doctrines of Calvinism and his zeal for evangelism. He believed that the doctrines of grace compelled believers to evangelism, knowing that only the Holy Spirit could bring souls to faith. In his introduction to a biography on evangelist Asahel Nettleton, Bonar wrote concerning the doctrines of grace, "Most assuredly they are fitted to lead a man and a minister of Christ (witness Dr. Nettleton) to be zealous of good works, and zealous for souls—bent upon God's glory, and bent upon the salvation of men…. Yes; *we work*, and pray, and travail for souls, because *God worketh* to will and to do His good pleasure."[10]

Andrew Bonar seemed to live for the privilege of evangelism. When his closest friend Robert Murray M'Cheyne died, he wrote, "My heart is sore. It makes me feel death near myself now. Life has lost half its joys, were it not for

---

9. A. A. Bonar, *Sheaves*, 78.

10. Bennet Tyler and Andrew A. Bonar, *Nettleton and His Labors* (Edinburgh: Banner of Truth, 1996), xv, xvi.

the hope of saving souls."[11] Bonar's spiritual edge stayed sharp by his focus on the gospel and the privilege of sharing it with others.

Sharing the Gospel with Children

Andrew Bonar's passion for seeing souls brought to Christ continued throughout his life and was especially seen in his love for communicating the gospel to children. In 1864 he used his "leisure moments" to write a book called *Palestine for the Young*. His desire in writing it was to teach the young about biblical places and "to show saving truth in connection with cities and country."[12] In his tract *The True Heaven and the Way to It*, Bonar stressed the joys of salvation and the importance of coming to Christ while still young: "Now, young friends, for whom I write, I would fain teach you from this subject some lessons.... You know that you are not too young to believe in Christ and be His children.... You will never regret coming to Christ in your youth." How do youth come to Christ? He stressed that they must not trust in their goodness but rather place faith in Jesus: "The soul lets go all other ways of trying to get God's favor...[and] agrees to take Jesus and his finished work."[13] He urges youth to "be pleased with him and rest on him alone, for favour with God." Bonar's tract *The Twelve Stones of Gilgal* is addressed to "Sabbath scholars." He teaches the young from Joshua 4, where Joshua called

---

11. M. Bonar, *Diary and Life*, 69.

12. M. Bonar, *Diary and Life*, 167.

13. A. A. Bonar, *Martyrs*.

twelve men to each take a stone out of the Jordan. This was to remind them of God's miracle in cutting off the waters of the Jordan so that His people could pass safely through with the ark of the covenant. Bonar explains that "Christ is our ark" and proceeds to share the gospel from this Old Testament account. He urged the young to waste no time in deciding to follow Christ: "You must not lose time in deciding," and again, "Young friend, you do not intend to be lost, but Satan intends to deceive you."[14]

The Lord's Return

Andrew Bonar's urgency in evangelism was directly related to his joyful anticipation of the Lord's return. The second coming of Christ was a vital theme for Bonar. He held firmly to his belief in the premillennial return of Christ, putting him at odds with the views of many in the Free Church of Scotland. While a student, Bonar had attended lectures on the subject by Edward Irving, and he had become convinced that the premillennial advent was a thoroughly scriptural doctrine.[15] While Irving would later fall into disrepute over other teachings, Bonar felt his views on eschatology were sound. The doctrine of the second coming shaped Bonar's life and fueled his zeal for sharing the message of God's salvation with others. Bonar had two inscriptions on the walls of his study: "Behold I come quickly" and "Even so come Lord Jesus."[16] He kept

---

14. A. A. Bonar, *The Twelve Stones of Gilgal*, in *Bonar Collection*.

15. Ferguson, *Rev. A. A. Bonar*, 85.

16. Ferguson, *Rev. A. A. Bonar*, 85.

these words ever before him as reminders of the need to live in a state of expectant readiness.

Andrew Bonar set forth his premillennial views on the second coming of Christ in his book *Redemption Drawing Nigh*, published in 1847. His evangelistic zeal flows throughout the book, viewing the second coming as a doctrine that should lead to urgency in evangelism. Concerning the need to present the gospel, he wrote, "Each believing man, as well as minister, is commanded to press this offer on the perishing world, while going onward to his rest. We are not to enter glory alone. Each of us must seek to bring in whom we can. The remembrance of the Lord's coming should have this effect upon us."[17]

Bonar thought that focusing on the second coming could yield a better understanding of the first coming. Concerning the second advent of Christ, he added, "It leads us to the First Coming. It fixes attention upon what the Gospel really is. It proclaims, 'He shall send Jesus Christ, which before was preached unto you' (Acts iii 20). Our attention is drawn to the person of Jesus. We are directed to One who is to come; and this is that same Jesus to whom sinners are directed now for their salvation."[18]

Bonar was not focused on the setting of dates or identifying of signs but rather on the person of Jesus Christ. His love for the doctrine of the second advent was based on his love for his Lord. He continued, "Now, in habitually contemplating the Second Coming of the Lord, our

17. A. A. Bonar, *Redemption*, 8.
18. A. A. Bonar, *Redemption*, 9.

eye is fixed on the person of Jesus; our soul is arrested, not by abstract truths, but by a living Person. The God-man who comes is the grand object that fills the soul. Is not this the very position of faith? And is not everything important that strengthens this habit of gazing on the Person of Christ?"[19]

Later, Bonar noted the importance of having one's faith strengthened in this way as he quoted his friend Robert Murray M'Cheyne: "O, my friends, your faith is incomplete if you do not live in the daily faith of a coming Saviour."[20]

Here lies the reason for Andrew Bonar's emphasis on the second coming of Christ. His preoccupation was not with a doctrine but with a person. He yearned for his readers and hearers to know and love the person of Jesus and thereby grow stronger in faith.

This emphasis on the person of Jesus was central to Bonar's understanding of the gospel as well as his emphasis on the second coming. He wrote, "The history of all God's holy love is there—in Him. And what we sometimes call real and vital *religion* is, properly and truly, acquaintance with Him, a true and vital acquaintance. All is made to centre in the person of Christ."[21] Bonar notes that this is the real key to assurance—knowing and relying on the person of Jesus: "Fixing his whole soul on Immanuel himself, the believer finds therein such abundant

---

19. A. A. Bonar, *Redemption*, 9–10.

20. A. A. Bonar, *Redemption*, 162.

21. A. A. Bonar, *Redemption*, 11.

proof of God's ability to clear away the guilt of the guilty as gives his soul deep, deep rest. *In the act of looking on the Saviour*, he sees 'peace in heaven and glory in the highest' (Luke xix.38)."[22]

22. A. A. Bonar, *Redemption*, 13.

Chapter 3

Humility, Compassion, and Servanthood

The most evident feature of Andrew Bonar's life was his humility. Bonar was a widely published author and was considered by many to be a biblical scholar. He pastored a large church and was elected the moderator of the Free Church of Scotland. He was a good friend of the world-famous D. L. Moody and had traveled to the United States at Moody's invitation. Yet none of his accomplishments seemed to puff him up with pride. Those who knew him best were often impressed with his genuine humility. After his death, Dr. William Laughton, a friend who had known him for over sixty years, said,

> I think I have never known anyone in public life so free from vanity, ostentation and the desire of applause.... I have known people who had much respect for him, express the utmost surprise, when told that he had occupied the foremost place, and carried off the highest prizes both at school and college; that he was a distinguished classical scholar, and that in his exact acquaintance with Scripture in the original language he had few equals, among those entirely devoted to the work of the ministry. As life advanced, his name was known and honoured, not only throughout the church to which he belonged, but among Evangelical Christians

of all denominations at home and abroad. But amid all
the distinction to which he attained it was true of him
to the last that he was "clothed with humility."[1]

Andrew Bonar's humility, while seen outwardly,
was shaped inwardly by his time alone with God. His
diary entries repeatedly testify that he was willing to be
unknown among people if he could know Christ more
fully. Early in his ministry he wrote, "This morning, after
much prayer, I was led to see that my present unhappiness rose from my unwillingness to be humbled and be
nothing. I desire now just to enjoy Christ as my Lord and
my Friend, and let Him send me among men, or keep me
unknown and unoccupied, as He pleases."[2]

Some years later, we see his continued struggle against
pride:

> Made to feel today, while here at Greenock commu-
> nion, the sin of desiring to be great and to have a name
> among men. Christ did not so desire. I have long had
> this sin to strive against. Today I felt somewhat able to
> tell the Lord that now renounced it forever; and that I
> wish to live to Him and to not be at all distressed by
> being unnoticed by men. Lord, enable me to live under
> the smile of Thy love, willing not to be noticed upon
> earth, if so I may glorify Thee more.[3]

Purposeful repentance from pride and the pursuit of
humility continued throughout Andrew Bonar's life. At
the age of seventy-three, after reflecting on Luke 13:30

---

1. Ferguson, *Rev. A. A. Bonar*, 251–52.

2. M. Bonar, *Diary and Life*, 35.

3. M. Bonar, *Diary and Life*, 102.

("And indeed there are last who will be first, and there are first who will be last"), he wrote, "It seems to warn some of us older ministers that it may be we may become self-confident, thinking that because of the past time we must of course stand out still superior to others."[4] During the last year of his life, in 1892, these words were written in his diary: "Have been humbled, and have seen myself dreadfully behind in real love to the Lord, and in the blessing and apprehension of His love to us, as stated in John 3:16. My soul was in a state of pain today because of this discovery of my terrible shortcoming. It may be the Lord is preparing me for more usefulness. I know that I must 'decrease.'"[5]

For all of his accomplishments, including the growth of the church he served from a handful of people to almost one thousand, Bonar seemed to increase in humility throughout his life. He clearly recognized that humility was essential in the life of a follower of Jesus, and he knew that the awareness of our weaknesses was connected to preparation for "more usefulness." Bonar's example reminds us that Christian leaders must pursue deeper humility throughout life and that this pursuit is especially important if we should experience success in our service.

Compassion and Care for All

In a tribute after his death, another friend noted Bonar's humility toward all types of people: "He seemed almost

---

4. M. Bonar, *Diary and Life*, 252.
5. M. Bonar, *Diary and Life*, 283–84.

unconscious of any distinctions of caste or class. He would rather render service to the insignificant people, who could make him no return, than to those of wealth or position."[6]

Bonar's humble regard for all people is seen in a short book he wrote titled *The Brook Besor: Words for Those Who Must Tarry at Home*. The unusual title comes from the events of 1 Samuel 30, which took place while David was fleeing from King Saul. David and his band of warriors had established a makeshift camp at Ziklag, but while they were away, the Amalekites invaded and burned their camp, taking captive their families. David and his army of six hundred pursued the Amalekites until they reached the Brook Besor. Here, two hundred men, "who were so weary that they could not cross the Brook Besor," stayed behind (v. 10).

After David and his four hundred soldiers defeated the Amalekites and recovered their families and possessions, they returned to the Brook Besor. Some of those with David were determined not to share the recovered possessions with those who had remained behind. But David would have none of that: "My brethren, you shall not do so with what the LORD has given us, who has preserved us and delivered into our hand the troop that came against us. For who will heed you in this matter? But as his part is who goes down to the battle, so shall his part be who stays by the supplies; they shall share alike" (vv. 23–24).

In *The Brook Besor*, Andrew Bonar takes this account of David's compassion and generosity and applies it to those

---

6. Ferguson, *Rev. A. A. Bonar*, 242.

in the church who feel they are unable to make significant contributions to the Lord's work. The introduction to the book reads, "What is written here is for the lonely ones of God's people,—the sick, the weak, the obscure." Bonar directs the book to "those of God's family who may often think themselves overlooked, and who often fancy themselves useless in the Church." He especially notes his hope that it will be a help to "the lonely ones of God's people; to those who must 'tarry at home'; and to all who oftentimes mourn that they are not able to do work for God in the way others do."[7]

This little book is filled with encouragement for those who suffer physically or emotionally and consider their lives to be of little purpose. Bonar especially notes the value of praise on the part of those who suffer: "One note of praise from his lonely ones is as sweet to the Lord as the loud song of the great multitude in heaven."[8] He concludes the book with a series of short comments on sixty places in Scripture where the words "Fear not" are found, noting that each passage demonstrates "how greatly the faint and weary are cared for."[9] The whole book is a beautiful expression of concern for those who might otherwise be disregarded by church leaders.

It should not surprise us that Andrew Bonar would write a book focused on God's "lonely ones," because

7. Andrew A. Bonar, *The Brook Besor* (New York: Robert Carter and Brothers, 1880), 5–6.

8. A. A. Bonar, *Brook Besor*, 67.

9. A. A. Bonar, *Brook Besor*, 83.

he never seemed to consider himself above the lowliest believer. He seemed immune from the tendency to focus on church members with the greatest potential or capacity for giving. This is especially seen in the attention he gave to children. He never considered himself too old or dignified to treat children with the highest regard. Children seemed to be drawn to the gentle elderly man, and his countenance communicated love and acceptance toward them. Noting her father's care for children, Bonar's daughter, Marjory, wrote,

> Each had a place in his prayers, and they fully returned his affection. They would linger in the church as he went from the pulpit to the vestry, in the hope of having his hand laid on their head, and hearing him call them by their name. One little child called him "the minister with the laughing face." It was not uncommon in Collace to see groups of children round him as he rode about from place to place on his pony. One of the touching sights on the day on which he was buried, was that of the children round the grave, with their sad and wistful faces.[10]

It should be no surprise to us that one of Andrew Bonar's diary entries reads, "Came home from church accompanied by a band of children who sang hymn after hymn."[11]

---

10. M. Bonar, *The Good Pastor*, 67.
11. M. Bonar, *Diary and Life*, 146.

Servant, Not Celebrity

Andrew Bonar's deep humility and Christlike compassion were expressed in a life of servanthood. Regarding his pastoral ministry, his daughter wrote, "No service was too small for him to do for any of Christ's little ones, and the joy of his service was as remarkable as its ceaselessness. 'Love is the *motive* for working,' he used to say, 'joy is the *strength* for working.'"[12]

Bonar's servanthood and humility are seen in the books and tracts he chose to write. He never wrote an autobiography, but he authored several works about the lives of others. The best known of these is certainly his *Memoir and Remains of Robert Murray M'Cheyne*. But he also wrote the *Memoir of the Life and Brief Ministry of the Rev. David Sandeman, Missionary to China*.[13] He wrote the introduction to a book about evangelist Asahel Nettleton and helped to edit his biography.[14] He wrote the preface to a book about John Vassar, a man whom Bonar described as "a living fire."[15] He wrote the prefaces to two books related to Samuel Rutherford—one a compilation of his letters and the other a selection of his sermons.[16]

Several of Bonar's tracts were short biographical

12. M. Bonar, *Diary and Life*, 348.

13. Andrew Bonar, *Memoir of the Life and Brief Ministry of the Rev. David Sandeman, Missionary to China* (London: James Nisbet & Co., 1862; repr., Ithaca, N.Y.: Cornell University Press, 1997).

14. Tyler and Bonar, *Nettleton and His Labors*.

15. Andrew Bonar, preface to Thomas E. Vassar, *Uncle John Vassar: or, The Fight of Faith* (Charleston, S.C.: BiblioLife, n.d.).

16. Andrew Bonar, ed., *Letters of Samuel Rutherford* (1984; repr., Edinburgh: Banner of Truth, 2006).

sketches of spiritual heroes who might otherwise have been forgotten. The short biographies that were intended to teach spiritual truths include

> *Emilia Geddie—A Child of the Covenant, Who Died in 1681: An Example Alike to Young and Old*

> *The Monk of Inchcolm*

> *Story of Andrew Lindsay*

> *Joy in Christ: The Story of a Young Believer* (about a girl named Elizabeth Morrison)

> *The Hermit of Sinai: A Narrative from Church History in the Fifth Century*

> *The Martyrs by the Sea: The Story of the Wigtown Sufferers* (about two women who gave their lives for Christ)[17]

Bonar put significant effort into research for these tracts, believing the accounts of these otherwise unknown Christians had much to teach his contemporaries. It is notable that for all of his research and writing about others, he never wrote about himself. But this was typical of Andrew Bonar—thinking much of others and little of himself.

Bonar's servanthood was also seen in his role as a bridge builder who sought to unite Christians in order to spread the gospel and build God's kingdom. This is seen most clearly in his support of American evangelist D. L. Moody. The popular Moody was attracting large crowds throughout Great Britain, but not all of Bonar's

---

17. All are works appearing in *Bonar Collection*.

Free Church of Scotland contemporaries were support-ive of the uneducated American. However, like Barnabas with the apostle Paul, Bonar publicly showed his support for Moody and helped to further his evangelistic ministry throughout Scotland.[18]

Scottish pastor Alex Rattray recalled that Bonar enabled him to get a personal meeting with Moody. Rattray hoped to get answers to questions he had about Moody and "see what manner of man he was." But after the meeting, in which Bonar was an observer, Rattray recalled little about Moody and much about Bonar:

> Of all that was said at this meeting I am free to con-fess I cannot recall a single word. But this is what strikes me in looking back upon it. Here was a man considerably older than Mr. Moodie; a man of varied attainments; ripe scholarship; keen and discriminating intellect; a rich and discursive fancy, and underlying all and sanctifying all other gifts a long and deep experi-ence of spiritual things; a life-long endeavor to walk with God; not wholly in vain; and to me it was a beau-tiful and very touching thing to see such a man, thus hanging on the lips of the new Evangelist, with the eager timidity of a Neophyte, to whom everything was new and everything was wonderful. But this humility was just one of those characteristics of Dr. Bonar that made everybody love him.[19]

18. Lyle Dorsett, *A Passion for Souls: The Life of D. L. Moody* (Chicago: Moody Publishers, 1997).

19. Ferguson, *Rev. A. A. Bonar*, 192–93.

Chapter 4

————— ❧ —————

Bonar's Communion with God

Andrew Bonar's daily fellowship with the Lord kept his spiritual edge sharp, and his rich communion with God made his godliness visible to others. In a tribute written after Bonar's death, a friend wrote, "The great secret of his success in brightening and sweetening sin-cursed humanity was that he spent much time on the mountaintop with God, and was therefore successful with men in the valley below. Let young men take note: there is only one way to reach permanent success that will stand the fire of the world and the test of time, to be much alone with God."[1]

For Bonar, communion with God was the highest of privileges. He typically began his time alone with God in study and meditation of Scripture. This prepared him for prayer and the enjoyment of God's presence. And while friends admired the extent of Bonar's time "on the mountaintop with God," Bonar often seemed to think he needed to seek God more fully. He wrote, "God will not let me get the blessing without asking. Today I am setting my face to fast and pray for enlightenment and refreshing.

————————

1. Ferguson, *Rev. A. A. Bonar*, 270.

Until I can get up to the measure of at least two hours in *pure prayer* every day, I shall not be contented. Meditation and reading besides."[2]

Over time, Bonar came to learn that prayer must be joined with praise. In a sermon delivered at the Mildmay Conference, Bonar said, "Prayer must be followed by praise. Prayer by itself (the Lord seems to say) is very well, but He wants praise; He must have the harp as well as the golden vial full of odour. *We* must now have both, as well as those that stand before the Lamb."[3]

Andrew Bonar came to realize that his communion with God in prayer and praise was directly related to his power in preaching. He wrote, "God will not let me preach with power when I am not much with Him. More than ever do I feel that I should be as much an intercessor as a preacher of the Word. Also I have been taught that joy in the Spirit is the frame in which God blesses us with others. Joy arises from fellowship with Him."[4]

Bonar's dependence on prayer as essential to fruitfulness in ministry seemed to grow as the years passed. During his second and final pastorate in Glasgow, he wrote, "More and more do I learn that continual watchfulness unto prayer is essential to right preaching, right visiting, right conversation, right reading of the Word."[5] Several years later, he began the new year by noting "a deep

---

2. M. Bonar, *Diary and Life*, 60, 63.

3. A. A. Bonar, *Sheaves*, 13–14.

4. M. Bonar, *Diary and Life*, 86.

5. M. Bonar, *Diary and Life*, 210.

persuasion that I may be this year a great benefactor by praying much."[6]

The foremost benefit that Andrew Bonar anticipated from communion with God in prayer was joy in God's presence. Concerning this joy, Bonar held that "joy does not depend upon our having or wanting earthly things; it depends upon our fellowship with God."[7] Bonar understood this joy to be very different from what we often consider as happiness. A believer's joy is not based on circumstances or feelings. Our joy is grounded on the reality of God's presence, made real to us by the Holy Spirit. A believer's joy is marked by awe and reverence before our holy God. Bonar wrote, "Beware of familiarity in prayer and in using the Scriptures. We are apt to rush into God's presence. There ought to be an awe upon us, an awe of reverence, not fear nor bondage, but the Bethel-awe that Jacob had."[8]

This awe in God's presence changes us. His Spirit meets the deepest needs of our hearts and conforms us to His likeness at the same time. Bonar wrote, "God alone is sufficient to satisfy the craving of our heart. As we grow in experience of this, we grow in holiness."[9]

The benefits of rich communion with God go beyond the meeting of our deepest needs and shaping us toward joy-filled holiness. Our fellowship with the Lord empowers our witness to the world. Andrew Bonar's

6. M. Bonar, *Diary and Life*, 210.

7. Marjory Bonar, ed., *Wayside Wells* (London: Hodder and Stoughton, 1908), 100.

8. M. Bonar, *Wayside Wells*, 37.

9. M. Bonar, *Wayside Wells*, 74.

message titled "Communion with God" was based on
Exodus 34:29–30, the passage that describes the shining
face of Moses when he descended from Mount Sinai with
the Ten Commandments. Bonar imagines the communion that Moses enjoyed with God during forty days on
the mountain and notes the effect of that communion—
Moses's face was shining! Bonar goes on to assert that a
believer who enjoys close fellowship with the Lord will be
changed by that fellowship: "As the fruit of communion,
you will find the Holy Spirit has made your conscience
more tender, your heart more loving, and your life more
holy—your whole soul and being, thought, word, and
deed, more like your Master. Most blessed result surely of
communion with Him!"[10]

Bonar then asserts that a believer who enjoys close
communion with God may, in some instances, display the
effects of that communion outwardly as a witness to unbe-
lievers: "By your calm shining countenance you may be
used to awaken souls…. I believe we might awaken men
all around us by our very presence if we had nearer communion with God."[11]

To those who might scoff at his suggestion of a visible witness on a believer's countenance, Bonar pointed
to the biblical example of Stephen, whose face was like
"the face of an angel" while being persecuted (Acts 6:15).
Bonar also pointed to those affected by the presence of

---

10. Andrew A. Bonar, *From Strength to Strength* (London: Morgan
& Scott, n.d.), 27–28.

11. A. A. Bonar, *Strength to Strength*, 33.

his friend, Robert Murray M'Cheyne. One person told of having been "awakened not so much by what he said as by his whole appearance and tone—the calm holiness that seemed to shine in him." Another spoke to Bonar of M'Cheyne's impact on him "by the holy look and manner of that man of God, almost before he had uttered a sentence." Bonar concluded, "You see the power of communion and fellowship with God. If you live near to God your words will tell wonderfully upon people. No doubt you will repel some, but you will draw others."[12]

Before leaving the example of Moses's shining face, Bonar took care to note that "Moses did not know that the skin of his face shone because he had been talking with God" (see Ex. 34:29). He noted that Moses "was so engrossed by his communion with God that he spent no thought upon himself." Bonar then explained, "If you want to get the better of self this is the secret of it—be engrossed with fellowship with God. Nothing gives such a blow to self as this communion with God. You *will* be troubled with self in some form continually, but here is the remedy—more of communion with God. This is ever the way to reach real humility."[13]

It is noteworthy that Andrew Bonar's communion with God was based not on his feelings or emotions but on the certainty of God's presence with him in all of life's circumstances. His life was not an easy one. His daughter Marjory wrote, "Sorrow fell to his lot. Disappointment

---

12. A. A. Bonar, *Strength to Strength*, 35.
13. A. A. Bonar, *Strength to Strength*, 36–37.

chilled his hopes. Deeper waters crossed his pathway than even those nearest him ever knew."[14] Yet Andrew Bonar drew nearer to God during his times of grief and sorrow. In 1860, Bonar and his wife lost their son Andrew. Bonar's diary entries during that time reveal his pursuit of God during severe sorrow: "Last night sitting up expecting every moment that little Andrew would breathe his last. How such a time of sorrow tries the soul! Discovering the vanity of all but fellowship with God."[15]

Tragedy struck again in October 1864 when Bonar lost his beloved wife, Isabella. His diary again notes his turning to the Lord for His help during grief: "Lord, let me not love Thee less, but more, because of this stroke, and from this day may I work more for the ingathering of souls." His diary entry of the following day provides more detail:

> There are many praying for me, I know. It is a relief to me to write down a little of what I feel and see as the hours of this solemn, solemn day pass on. My dear boy James has been with me most of the day. They all feel their dear mother's loss, with bursting hearts, so that I cannot often bear to think upon their loss. My Lord and Saviour is henceforth to be to me instead of what I have lost.[16]

In the following days, Bonar wrote much about his wife. He noted,

> On looking back I can see very many lessons she has

---

14. Marjory Bonar, ed., *Reminiscences of Andrew A. Bonar D. D.* (London: Hodder and Stoughton, 1897), vii.

15. M. Bonar, *Diary and Life*, 148.

16. M. Bonar, *Diary and Life*, 169.

taught me as to how I should feel toward the Lord Jesus, and how truly He may come into the place which he has seen good to leave empty…. The torrent is now settling into a calm river. My soul is finding real sweetness in the Lord and in the hope set before me. Besides all which, the personal and direct presence of the Holy Ghost, the Comforter, has been in my soul.[17]

Here, Andrew Bonar reveals the most important key to his vibrant, soul-strengthening communion with God—a deep and reverent awareness of the presence of the Holy Spirit. Bonar seemed to live with a remarkable gratitude for this gift. In a message given at the Perth Convention in 1883, he said, "Shall we not honour and bless and adore the Holy Spirit? Surely it might well be expected that our love, our adoring and grateful love, should go forth to him to whom we owe so much; for every soul that has found the Saviour was brought to Him by the Holy Spirit."[18]

Bonar drew his comfort in sorrow and maintained close communion with God by his reliance on the Holy Spirit. Author Iain Murray notes that Andrew Bonar was very certain about how communion with God was to be maintained: "It is by the ministry of the Holy Spirit on God's part, and by prayer on our own. His *Diary* shows he regarded prayer as his main work, and among his prayers the most frequent was for the Holy Spirit to make the person and glory of Christ more real to him."[19]

17. M. Bonar, *Diary and Life*, 170–71.

18. A. A. Bonar, *Sheaves*, 62.

19. Iain H. Murray, *Seven Leaders* (Edinburgh: Banner of Truth, 2017), 62.

Murray explains that Bonar advised Christians to follow the pattern of the apostle Paul's prayers found in his New Testament letters. Bonar's favorite seems to have been the prayer found in Ephesians 3:16–19:

> That He would grant you, according to the riches of His glory, to be strengthened with might through His Spirit in the inner man, that Christ may dwell in your hearts through faith; that you, being rooted and grounded in love, may be able to comprehend with all the saints what is the width and length and depth and height—to know the love of Christ which passes knowledge; that you may be filled with all the fullness of God.

Andrew Bonar's emphasis on walking in step with the Holy Spirit was directly related to his emphasis on evangelism and the need for revival. In a message given at the Glasgow Christian Convention, Bonar called Christians to give up lesser things and to devote more time to praying for a great work of the Holy Spirit: "Leave off other reading. Leave off other employments. Give up some of your work, and pray down the Spirit that we may have a great Pentecostal blessing. Our only hope is in the Holy Spirit. Eloquence will not move a man's conscience nor will intellectual power. It is the Spirit that we need, the outpouring of the Holy Spirit."[20]

Bonar knew that revival begins with the work of the Holy Spirit in believers, and then He works through them to reach the unconverted. In a message titled "The Holy

20. A. A. Bonar, *Sheaves*, 39.

Spirit Convincing," Bonar said, "Revivals begin with God's own people; and the Holy Spirit touches their hearts anew, and gives them new fervour and compassion, and zeal, new light and life, and when He has thus come to you, He next goes forth to the valley of dry bones."[21]

Andrew Bonar was not known as an especially gifted preacher. His gifts did not include "a natural eloquence of speech and an appealing voice."[22] Those who knew him noted that who he was spoke far more loudly than what he did. Rev. S. Duff described Bonar as "a man of saintly and strong character, full of the Holy Spirit," and wrote, "The man himself was greater than anything he could have done or spoken."[23]

Another wrote, "His greatest ministry was his life. Men felt he lived the Gospel both in its spirit and law. His words, his looks, his magnetic influence were a perpetual sermon."[24]

The Glasgow United Evangelistic Association Bulletin included these words of tribute at Bonar's death:

> There was something about him singularly amiable and attractive—a most loveable man, full of the milk of human kindness.
>
> I think I have never known anyone in public life so free from vanity, ostentation and the desire of applause.
>
> But amid all the distinction to which he attained it

21. A. A. Bonar, *Sheaves*, 77.

22. Murray, *Seven Leaders*, 61.

23. Ferguson, *Rev. A. A. Bonar*, 161.

24. Ferguson, *Rev. A. A. Bonar*, 257.

was true of him to the last that he was "clothed with humility."[25]

While Andrew Bonar would never have agreed with such statements about himself, he would have strongly agreed that the Holy Spirit is the great shaper of our lives. He wrote, "If we are filled with the Spirit, God will bless everything about us, the tones of our voice, even the putting out of our hand."[26] Bonar also knew that the shaping work of the Holy Spirit often occurs as we pursue communion with God: "In prayer in the wood for some time, having set apart three hours for devotion; felt drawn out much to pray for that peculiar fragrance which believers have about them, who are very much in fellowship with God. It is like an aroma, unseen but felt."[27]

---

25. Ferguson, *Rev. A. A. Bonar*, 249–52.

26. M. Bonar, *Diary and Life*, 134.

27. Marjory Bonar, ed., *Heavenly Springs* (Edinburgh: Banner of Truth, 1986), 98.

Chapter 5

Learning from Andrew Bonar

Andrew Bonar was an exceptional leader because of his walk with God. He was not an especially gifted speaker. He was not as well known as his brother, Horatius, or as his good friend, Robert Murray M'Cheyne. His eschatological views put him in the minority among his fellow pastors. And his daughter notes that he was prone to depression. In his diary, he often laments his perceived lack of fruitfulness in ministry. Yet despite these things, his life shone with the brightness of God's presence. The fact that he was so ordinary was eclipsed by his nearness to God. By his communion with God, his greatest ministry became his life itself. Bonar's determination to keep his spiritual edge teaches us how an ordinary Christian leader can have an extraordinary walk with God. His example shows us how we can walk increasingly closely with the Lord over time. Here are seven lessons from Andrew Bonar's life that can help us do that.

Communion with God Should Be Our Highest Goal

Bonar's life teaches us that our fellowship with God should be an end in itself. We should pursue communion with the Lord for no higher purpose than to know Him better and love Him more. Understanding this can lead to a growing love for prayer.

Bonar's life of prayer grew as he learned to enjoy God's presence. Hearers remembered him saying, "Pray much and you will be very near the King, for He has a special love to petitions."[1] It was enjoyment of this nearness to God that compelled Bonar to pray. His life illustrates the truth that prayer is the primary way believers enjoy communion with God. Shaped by Scripture and empowered by the Holy Spirit, prayer is the avenue for experiencing God's nearness. This enjoyment of God's presence can be the greatest enduring motivation for a life of prayer.

There is much to be learned by observing Bonar's communion with God during suffering. In his most severe times of grief, Bonar did not turn away from the Lord but instead drew near to Him. It has been said that the hearts of some people are like clay and the hearts of others are like wax. When the heat of adversity or suffering comes, the hearts of some are hardened, becoming resistant to God and His ways. But the hearts of others are softened during adversity. They draw near to God. They become more malleable and are more conformed to His likeness through suffering. Andrew Bonar was of this latter type.

By his example and teaching, Andrew Bonar reminds us that believers must not become complacent about their fellowship with the Lord. In a sermon delivered shortly before his death, he warned that "some disciples cool down

---

1. M. Bonar, *Diary and Life*, 337.

and are not as when they began. Be not of that number though MANY such be around you."[2]

Andrew Bonar's life shows us that extraordinary gifts and abilities are not necessary for one to enjoy an extraordinary life of communion with God. We don't have to be like the "many" who lose their spiritual edge. Our spiritual vitality and love for our Lord can grow throughout our lives. Like Bonar, we can go from strength to strength.

> Blessed is the man whose strength is in You,
> Whose heart is set on pilgrimage.
> As they pass through the Valley of Baca,
> They make it a spring;
> The rain also covers it with pools.
> They go from strength to strength;
> Each one appears before God in Zion. (Ps. 84:5–7)

The Richness of Scripture Compels Us to Be Lifelong Learners

Andrew Bonar's life reminds us that the sixty-six books of the Bible are worthy of a lifetime of diligent study. His example further reminds us that all Scripture is inspired by God—the Old as well as the New Testament.

In recent years, a well-known American pastor encouraged Christians to "unhitch" from the Old Testament. Apparently, he felt that the Old Testament could present a hindrance in sharing the gospel with non-Christians. Andrew Bonar would have strongly disagreed—as should

---

2. Ferguson, *Rev. A. A. Bonar*, 283.

we! Bonar would have explained that the Old Testament leads us to Christ.

After Bonar's death, a friend's tribute to him read, "Always expository, he had a happy way of connecting together the truths of the Old and New Testaments, and of bringing out their more hidden spiritual meanings and of applying them to the varied experiences and conditions and circumstances of the hearers."[3]

This observation is proven true by the many messages Bonar gave on little-known parts of the Bible. One example is his book titled *The Brook Besor*, from 1 Samuel 30. Others are his messages titled "The Cloak Left at Troas" and "A Little Wine" (based on 2 Tim. 4:13 and 1 Tim. 5:23, respectively). He also spoke on "The Pins of the Tabernacle" (Num. 3:37) and "The Napkin about Christ's Head" (John 20:7). It is no surprise that Marjory Bonar writes that her father would often say, "Notice the *little* things in the Bible."[4]

Andrew Bonar's thirst for learning was not limited to Scripture. His tracts reveal his interest in church history dating to the fifth century. His knowledge of theology was such that many considered him a scholar. And he especially enjoyed learning from the lives of Christians who had walked closely with Christ. Just prior to his eightieth birthday, Bonar finished an edition of *Samuel Rutherford's Letters*. Regarding his work on that volume, Bonar wrote, "Got much from it to my own soul all the time; the

---

3. Ferguson, *Rev. A. A. Bonar*, 200.
4. M. Bonar, *Diary and Life*, 402.

love of Christ that filled his heart throws out its sparks as we read."[5]

It is tempting for those with years of experience in teaching and preaching to rely on knowledge gained in the past. When we have read through the Bible numerous times, we may be tempted to complacency in our study. But Andrew Bonar's example reminds us that the riches of God's Word are inexhaustible. The gift of Scripture calls us to a lifetime of joyful study and growing knowledge of the One whom it reveals.

Intercessory Prayer Should Be a Significant Ministry for Any Christian Leader

Those of us who are pastors often consider preaching, and the study it requires, to be our most important work, and rightly so. We sometimes point to Acts 6:2, which records the apostles saying, "It is not desirable that we should leave the word of God and serve tables." But we may neglect an important part of the commitment made by the apostles: "But we will give ourselves continually to prayer and to the ministry of the word" (Acts 6:4). For the apostles, prayer was prioritized along with the ministry of preaching. The two should never be separated.

Andrew Bonar's view was that prayer was essential if one's ministry of preaching was to be effective. He understood that the Holy Spirit must empower preaching for it to be fruitful and that the Spirit's power was present when prayer was plentiful. He wrote, "My chief desire should

5. M. Bonar, *Diary and Life*, 279.

be on this day to be a man of prayer, for there is no want of speaking and writing and preaching and teaching and warning; but there is need of the Holy Spirit to make all this effectual."[6]

Bonar felt it especially important to pray for the people to whom he ministered. He noted the example of the apostle Paul and his ministry of intercessory prayer: "Paul found time, in the midst of a thousandfold more to occupy him, to pray for individual cases often and much. Prayer should make time for itself."[7]

Bonar makes the excellent point that the apostle Paul, with the many churches and people for whom he provided discipleship, prayed much for those he served. It is remarkable to read Paul's letters to the churches and to note how frequently he prayed for them. Passages like Ephesians 1:16–19 and 3:14–21, Philippians 1:9–11, Colossians 1:9–11, 1 Thessalonians 1:2–3, 2 Thessalonians 1:11–12, and 2 Timothy 1:3 remind us that the apostle Paul was an intercessor. He prayed much for God's work in the lives of the people to whom he ministered.

Church leaders today often make the mistake of relegating intercessory prayer in the church to a few "prayer warriors" who are noted for their interest in praying. But rather than viewing prayer as a ministry for a select few, we should see prayer as the fuel for all ministry. Perhaps then we would see a greater working of the Holy Spirit in all areas of church life and ministry. Perhaps we would

---

6. M. Bonar, *Diary and Life*, 102.
7. M. Bonar, *Diary and Life*, 196.

find what Andrew Bonar said to be true: "If we prayed more, we should not have to work so hard."[8]

The Purposeful Pursuit of Holiness Is Essential for a Genuinely Fruitful Ministry

Many people have a vague understanding of holiness as something defined by things a person does or does not do. Andrew Bonar reminds us that Scripture provides us a better understanding: holiness is likeness to Jesus Christ. Bonar said, "It is not ceasing to do evil and learning to do well that sanctifies us. It is breathing the atmosphere of the love of Christ."[9]

Biblical holiness is not seen in our rule keeping but in our being conformed to the likeness of Jesus Christ (Rom. 8:29). Holiness is seen when a person is filled with the Holy Spirit. The fruit of the Spirit (Gal. 5:22–23) will be abundant in the life of a holy person. That is why Bonar could say, "You are not very holy if you are not very kind."[10]

Andrew Bonar's understanding of the way to greater holiness was undoubtedly shaped by the teaching of one of his most influential instructors—Thomas Chalmers, a professor of theology at the University of Edinburgh. Chalmers's approach to holiness is revealed in one of his best-known messages, *The Expulsive Power of a New Affection.*[11] Chalmers made the points that "such is the grasping

---

8. M. Bonar, *Wayside Wells*, 65.

9. M. Bonar, *Heavenly Springs*, 102.

10. M. Bonar, *Reminiscences*, 125.

11. Thomas Chalmers, *The Expulsive Power of a New Affection* (Minneapolis, Minn.: Curiosmith, 2012).

tendency of the human heart, that it must have something
to lay hold of" and that "the only way to dispossess it of an
old affection, is by the expulsive power of a new one."[12] He
went on to explain that

> the best way of casting out an impure affection is to
> admit a pure one; and by the love of what is good, to
> expel the love of what is evil. Thus it is, that the freer
> the gospel, the more sanctifying is the gospel; and the
> more it is received as a doctrine of grace, the more will
> it be felt as a doctrine according to godliness.[13]

Chalmers concluded that the believer who understands
the greatness of God's grace in the gospel will embrace a
higher love than love of sin. Love for God expels all lesser
loves.

It was this greater love that compelled Andrew Bonar
to the ongoing pursuit of greater likeness to Christ. He
wrote, "When the Lord is with us in His fulness it is the
ocean sweeping away all that was unholy, and bringing in
all that is pure. Every craving of the soul is met and filled."[14]

Bonar understood that the Holy Spirit is the great
shaper of our lives and the One who guides our progress
in holiness. The more we humbly yield to His presence,
the more we will be conformed to the likeness of Christ.
This shaping of our lives is critically important to the fruitfulness of our ministries. Andrew Bonar never stopped
seeking the Spirit's fullness for a more holy and empow-

---

12. Chalmers, *Expulsive Power*, 12.
13. Chalmers, *Expulsive Power*, 27–28.
14. M. Bonar, *Diary and Life*, 239.

ered life. He wrote, "Lord, before I finish my course, may I reach further into the mystery of Godliness, and have more power with Thee to bring down blessing on earth."[15] May we have this same desire!

A Leader's Life Should Be One of Humble Servanthood

Andrew Bonar's example reminds us that Christian leadership is more about who we are than what we accomplish. Our leadership strength is perhaps best seen in the genuineness of our humility. Jesus reminded us that true greatness is seen in servanthood and humility when He said, "But he who is greatest among you shall be your servant. And whoever exalts himself will be humbled, and he who humbles himself will be exalted" (Matt. 23:11–12).

In a message titled "The Pins of the Tabernacle," Bonar spoke about the pins and cords that were under the charge of the sons of Merari (Num. 3:36–37). These priests were appointed to carry tent pegs and other accessories while the sons of Kohath were charged with the ark itself. Bonar imagines the sons of Merari complaining:

> "Why do our brethren the Kohathites carry the Ark?" *Because God said it*; that is all. He that serves most is greatest in the kingdom. He who carries the pins may get the greatest reward.... If you get out of the rut of carrying pins when God put you there, you will not be blessed. Are we in the camp with God? That is the great thing.[16]

---

15. M. Bonar, *Diary and Life*, 221.
16. M. Bonar, *Reminiscences*, 286–88.

Bonar's point is that a hidden ministry of faithful service may be more pleasing to God than a more prominent ministry pursued apart from the Lord's guidance. Being where God calls us to be is more important than any degree of public recognition. God blesses faithful work done in response to His calling.

Bonar's diary reveals that he sometimes compared his ministry with that of others and lamented what he perceived to be a lesser degree of God's blessing on his preaching. Yet his consistent example teaches us that genuine leaders should not be self-promoters, but those who put the interests of others before their own (Phil. 2:4). We are called to follow the example of the One who "did not come to be served, but to serve" (Matt. 20:28).

Bonar's humility and desire to serve were especially seen in his care for God's "lonely ones." *The Brook Besor* reveals his special compassion for those with physical or mental disabilities and those who feel that they have little to offer in service to God's kingdom. His life reminds us that leaders should pay special attention to "the least of these My brethren" (Matt. 25:40). Bonar also taught us much about servanthood by the great attention he gave to children. He seemed to feel a special urgency about reaching them with the gospel, as is evidenced by his many evangelistic tracts written for the young. His example is of special importance to church leaders who are often tempted to focus only on those who can give, serve, or influence decisions in the church. We must consider Jesus's response when His disciples sought to deter parents from bringing their children to Him: "Let the little children come to Me, and do not forbid them; for of such is the kingdom of heaven" (Matt. 19:14). Andrew Bonar's example reminds us that Christlike leaders care deeply about children and "the least of these."

Today's church world is filled with examples of leaders who have overseen large and prominent ministries at the cost of their own humility and servanthood. Popularity is a dangerous thing for a Christian leader. If we should experience growth and evidence of God's blessing in our ministries, we would do well to remember Andrew Bonar's prayer: "That God has used me is nothing else than the merest sovereign grace."[17]

We Should Live in Expectation of the Second Coming of Christ

Andrew Bonar wrote, "No Christian denies the fact of the Second Coming of Christ. But very many, even of the most godly in the later days, have failed to meditate much upon this blessed hope. It has been left, like an old sword, looked at and its properties occasionally descanted upon, but unused by Christ's soldiers in battle."[18]

Bonar laments the fact that many in his time neglected to focus on the second coming. While not all would share his premillennial views, he felt that all ministers, especially, should emphasize Christ's return. Bonar's concerns could easily be applied to our time, and his reasons for

17. M. Bonar, *Diary and Life*, 247.
18. A. A. Bonar, *Redemption*, 33.

emphasizing the "blessed hope" can bring spiritual health and renewal to us today.

Bonar reminds us that the expectation of Christ's return calls us to holiness. He notes that "TRUE HOLINESS cannot be fully cultivated apart from this realized hope."[19] As support for his claim, Bonar pointed to Titus 2:11–13: "For the grace of God that brings salvation has appeared to all men, teaching us that, denying ungodliness and worldly lusts, we should live soberly, righteously, and godly in the present age, looking for the blessed hope and glorious appearing of our great God and Savior Jesus Christ." It is by "looking for" the glorious return of Christ that we experience God's enabling grace to live more holy lives.

The apostle Paul elsewhere calls believers to avoid the ungodliness of those who set their minds on "earthly things" and to live as those whose "citizenship is in heaven, from which we also eagerly wait for the Savior, the Lord Jesus Christ" (Phil. 3:19–20). Writing to the church at Colossae, Paul called Christians to set their minds on things above and to "put to death" earthly sins in light of the coming appearance of Christ (Col. 3:2–5). The apostle Peter writes of the certainty of "the day of the Lord" and calls believers to "holy conduct and godliness" in light of Christ's return (2 Peter 3:10–12). The apostle John provides a wonderful promise for the one who lives in expectation of Jesus's return: "And everyone who has this hope in Him purifies himself, just as He is pure" (1 John 3:3).

Bonar believed that emphasizing the second coming

---

19. A. A. Bonar, *Redemption*, 36.

could give urgency to evangelism. It could stir believers to action in sharing the gospel with others, and it could help call sinners to the awareness of their need for salvation. Bonar wrote, "For it is a doctrine well fitted to arouse from sleep, like the cry of a shipmaster to Jonah; and well fitted to direct attention to the simple Gospel, by fixing the sinner's eye on Christ's person, the God-man."[20]

Bonar's association of the second coming with urgency in evangelism reminds us of Peter's words in 2 Peter 3:9–10: "The Lord is not slack concerning His promise, as some count slackness, but is longsuffering toward us, not willing that any should perish but that all should come to repentance. But the day of the Lord will come as a thief in the night." Note Peter's words that the Lord is longsuffering *toward us*. We who know the Lord are to be zealous for evangelism in light of Jesus's return.

Andrew Bonar's example teaches us that the second coming of Christ calls us to spiritual alertness. We are to live in readiness by drawing on God's grace for holiness. We are to rely on the Holy Spirit for compassion for the lost and power in evangelism. We should live in joyful expectation of Christ's return.

"Even so, come, Lord Jesus!" (Rev. 22:20).

We Should Grow Closer to God as We Age

Andrew Bonar seemed to remember well the advice from an older minister that was given to him earlier in life: "Remember, it is a remark of old and experienced men,

---

20. A. A. Bonar, *Redemption*, 39–40.

that very few men, and very few *ministers*, keep up to the end the edge that was on their spirit at the first."[21]

Bonar was aware that spiritual complacency and self-confidence could stifle continued zeal and growing communion with God later in life. When he was seventy-three years old, he wrote in his diary, "Startled while reading Luke 13:30. It seems to warn some of us older ministers that it may be we may become self-confident, thinking that because of the past time, we must of course stand out still superior to others."[22]

Bonar was aware that his age could certainly bring changes in his level of activity and almost certainly to ministry requiring travel. But he saw no need to ever decrease in prayer and the enjoyment of God's presence. At age seventy-seven he wrote, "I have been led to inquire if perhaps it may be the Lord's will to use me in my old age rather for prayer and praise than for direct work."[23]

Regardless of the form his ministry would take, Bonar expected to continue to bear fruit. At age eighty he wrote, "In our younger days a great deal is *blossom*, but as we grow older it is *fruit*. It does not make such an appearance, but it is more enduring."[24]

Andrew Bonar's life reminds us that we should never stop growing to know God better and love Him more. By our fellowship with God, we can "go from strength to

---

21. M. Bonar, *Diary and Life*, 252.

22. M. Bonar, *Diary and Life*, 252.

23. M. Bonar, *Diary and Life*, 263.

24. M. Bonar, *Diary and Life*, 384.

strength" (Ps. 84:7). As Psalm 71:18 reminds us, even when "old and grayheaded," we can be used by God to declare His power to those who will follow us. Those who have embraced the gift of righteousness provided by Jesus Christ can be like the righteous who "still bear fruit in old age; they shall be fresh and flourishing" (Ps. 92:14).

Our bodies will age. Our vocations and ministries may change. But we need never stop walking closely with God. As Bonar's life reminds us, we can keep our spiritual edge.

————— ❧·❧ —————

Wisdom from Bonar

Communion with God

But is it not intimated to us by there being such a book as "The Song of Songs" that the Lord desires far more of our communion with Him than we generally relish?[1]

Our first and all-including loss by the Fall, was loss of communion with God. But all we lost the Lord restores to us in redemption.[2]

And this very great lesson I have so far learned, that God alone, in the absence of friends, with none to sympathize, can be the joy and portion of my soul.[3]

I must seek this day to live more every hour in communion with Christ; never to be hasty or vain in my conversation; oftener to be alone with God; pray more for conversions.[4]

1. Andrew A. Bonar, *The Gospel Pointing to the Person of Christ* (Edinburgh: Andrew Stevenson, 1888), 81.

2. A. A. Bonar, *Sheaves*, 118.

3. M. Bonar, *Diary and Life*, 32.

4. M. Bonar, *Diary and Life*, 40.

I learned much from [M'Cheyne], especially and chiefly from his recollectedness of soul and nearness of communion with God.[5]

I see, too, that to be close with God gives abundant strength, and is like light shining upon a gloomy country in summertime; it makes things look different indeed.[6]

I see plainly that *fellowship with God is not means to an end*, but is to be *the end itself*.[7]

God will not let me preach with power when I am not much with Him.[8]

Nothing satisfies the whole soul but the Lord himself.[9]

I am persuaded that the other world is in a measure felt when a soul is truly in the act of communion with the Lord.[10]

It is not simply the being cumbered with many things and troubled that hinders blessing; it is my being taken up with, and deeply interested in, many things that are not directly the Lord himself. Whereas the Lord himself is the one thing, fellowship with Him, delighting ourselves in Him.[11]

---

5. M. Bonar, *Diary and Life*, 43.
6. M. Bonar, *Diary and Life*, 62.
7. M. Bonar, *Diary and Life*, 76.
8. M. Bonar, *Diary and Life*, 86.
9. M. Bonar, *Diary and Life*, 93.
10. M. Bonar, *Diary and Life*, 108.
11. M. Bonar, *Diary and Life*, 143.

My heart's desire is that the sweetness of divine communion may to me be such that it will make all other wants forgotten.[12]

I see that I will need every day more and more in the morning before any business begins, a cup of the new wine of the kingdom—fellowship with God.[13]

You need hourly fellowship with Christ, and to have this you must be watchful.[14]

The blood gives the conscience rest, but the heart craves something more, and that is fellowship with Him who gave us the atoning blood and sprinkled it on our souls.[15]

May we so enjoy communion with Thee that when we lose it we may feel just as if we were away from our home.[16]

In prayer in the wood for some time, having set apart three hours for devotion; felt drawn out much to pray for that peculiar fragrance which believers have about them, who are very much in fellowship with God. It is like an aroma, unseen but felt.[17]

The believer must never undervalue the sensible comforts of God's presence and fellowship.[18]

---

12. M. Bonar, *Diary and Life*, 229.
13. M. Bonar, *Heavenly Springs*, 23.
14. M. Bonar, *Heavenly Springs*, 24.
15. M. Bonar, *Heavenly Springs*, 64.
16. M. Bonar, *Heavenly Springs*, 85.
17. M. Bonar, *Heavenly Springs*, 98.
18. M. Bonar, *Wayside Wells*, 171.

If God is to guide us we must be in fellowship with Him.[19]

Keep a firm hold of that word "with one," for your sanctification. Remember it in our daily life. One with Christ and in fellowship with Him—in union with Him, and in holy communion with Him—what are difficulties to you?[20]

Evangelism

We are not to enter glory alone. Each of us must seek to bring in whom we can. The remembrance of the Lord's coming should have this effect upon us.[21]

This is a very solemn truth for the Church of God. And at the same time it is a wonderful privilege that is involved in this truth. We are honoured to do what angels are not; saints are they who are sent in the footsteps of the Son of Man to seek and save the lost.[22]

We need the blessed art of constantly bringing the Master into the foreground, never letting ourselves be thought of as any other than disciples whose anxiety is to commend the Master.[23]

---

19. M. Bonar, *Wayside Wells*, 181.
20. Ferguson, *Rev. A. A. Bonar*, 276 (sermon by Bonar shortly before his death).
21. A. A. Bonar, *Redemption*, 8.
22. A. A. Bonar, *Sheaves*, 78.
23. A. A. Bonar, *Strength to Strength*, 63.

God has taken away my fears, giving me very deep interest in the eternal salvation of all. The greater my love to their souls becomes, the less I fear anything.[24]

He has brought me to care far less than ever in my life about temporal enjoyments, if only I may be an instrument of saving souls.[25]

Were I holier, the thought of the unsaved would thus come back upon me from hour to hour. Lord, fill me with the Holy Ghost and the mind of Christ.[26]

There is work to be done for God here which we can never do again, never in heaven. We are His servants to go with His message. It is His wise plan not to send angels to gather in sinners; they gather in the saints.[27]

Conversions go on very much according to how the saints live. If love waxes cold, iniquity will abound. Saints are responsible for souls being saved.[28]

If you shine as lights now, and cast your light on the shadows around you, you will hear of it in the ages to come. If you do not, God will get others to do it.[29]

Faith
I see that all departure from a living God is a species of unbelief, and proceeds directly from unbelief. I feel that

24. M. Bonar, *Diary and Life*, 33.
25. M. Bonar, *Diary and Life*, 35.
26. M. Bonar, *Diary and Life*, 194.
27. M. Bonar, *Wayside Wells*, 115.
28. M. Bonar, *Wayside Wells*, 151.
29. M. Bonar, *Diary and Life*, 321.

did I live in direct faith I would live also in perpetual fellowship with God.[30]

I see that faith is high just when our thoughts about our Lord himself are high and great and satisfying.[31]

Faith keeps us, but God keeps our faith.[32]

It is the man of faith who is the man of duty.[33]

Unbelief looks at the difficulty, and faith looks at God.[34]

God does not ask us to feel that everything is for the best, but He does ask us to believe it.[35]

Faith is not the price we pay for salvation; faith is receiving salvation.[36]

A man full of faith is a man who takes much from the giving Saviour.[37]

Faith fits for but does not exempt from trial.[38]

It is a mistake, an unbelieving mistake, to say you are alone.[39]

---

30. M. Bonar, *Diary and Life*, 80.
31. M. Bonar, *Diary and Life*, 236.
32. M. Bonar, *Diary and Life*, 331.
33. M. Bonar, *Heavenly Springs*, 24.
34. M. Bonar, *Heavenly Springs*, 67.
35. M. Bonar, *Heavenly Springs*, 78–79.
36. M. Bonar, *Wayside Wells*, 47.
37. M. Bonar, *Wayside Wells*, 68.
38. M. Bonar, *Wayside Wells*, 83.
39. M. Bonar, *Wayside Wells*, 95.

Faith makes a shield of Christ, not of itself.[40]

Faith does not look in; it looks out.[41]

Focusing on Christ

To see Him is to see the God of holy love putting Himself in a position wherein He might be able, justly and honourably, to save sinners. To see Him is to see *Godhead* finding a way of coming to sinners with open arms, and yet remaining as holy, and just, and true, as from all eternity.[42]

Right views of sin have a tendency to lead us to right views of the Person of the Saviour. But the converse also is true; right views of the Saviour's person lead to right views of sin.[43]

When we dwell on the Saviour's Person, we are in His company. Faith places us by His side, and shows us His glory, until what we see makes our heart burn within us.[44]

More than ever convinced that sanctification is carried on by the Spirit by means of our direct looking upon the face of Jesus hour by hour, not only once or twice a day.[45]

And when I am under temptation, one look upward to Christ secures the victory.[46]

---

40. M. Bonar, *Wayside Wells*, 155.
41. M. Bonar, *Wayside Wells*, 163.
42. A. A. Bonar, *Person of Christ*, 7.
43. A. A. Bonar, *Person of Christ*, 34.
44. A. A. Bonar, *Person of Christ*, 80.
45. M. Bonar, *Diary and Life*, 125.
46. M. Bonar, *Diary and Life*, 204.

Christ is more than ever precious to me in His atonement, righteousness, merit, heart. Nothing else satisfies me. I only yearn to know Him better and preach Him more fully. His Cross and His Crown never lose their attractiveness. Day by day He is my rest, my heaven.[47]

We do not need new swords, new spears, new arms. We only need more eye-salve to see Who is on our side.[48]

The man who sees Christ in life is sure to see Him in the valley of the shadow of death.[49]

Think upon the Lord while you can, and He will think upon you when you can't.[50]

Paul's experience was very much what he found in Christ, not what he found out about himself. This is the best of all experiences.[51]

We must exalt Christ so high as to get out of sight of ourselves in looking up to Him.[52]

Our standing fast is due to a living, interceding Saviour, and our eye must rest on Him in an hour of trial.[53]

Lift our eyes heavenward. Earthward is bad enough, but

47. M. Bonar, *Diary and Life*, 222.
48. M. Bonar, *Diary and Life*, 331.
49. M. Bonar, *Diary and Life*, 404.
50. M. Bonar, *Heavenly Springs*, 31.
51. M. Bonar, *Heavenly Springs*, 47.
52. M. Bonar, *Heavenly Springs*, 50.
53. M. Bonar, *Heavenly Springs*, 75.

inward is dreadful. Lift us heavenward to where Jesus sitteth on the right hand of God.[54]

My eye ought not now to look around for anything to stay me, but to look upward always for the glory there, and the Lord himself who is to lead me.[55]

This Communion morning got some view of how deep may be the holy peace of a soul that sees the vastness of the Saviour's grace.[56]

Dying is just more of Christ.[57]

Keep your eye of hope on the second coming of the Lord, while your eye of faith rests on his finished work.[58]

It exalts a man to exalt Christ. It is by the gospel of the grace of God brought home to us again and again that we are built up.[59]

Those who do not look at His sacrifice do not follow His example.[60]

Despair arises from looking away from the cross, and despair is death.[61]

---

54. M. Bonar, *Heavenly Springs*, 133.
55. M. Bonar, *Heavenly Springs*, 134.
56. M. Bonar, *Heavenly Springs*, 139.
57. M. Bonar, *Heavenly Springs*, 179.
58. M. Bonar, *Wayside Wells*, 24.
59. M. Bonar, *Wayside Wells*, 87.
60. M. Bonar, *Wayside Wells*, 88.
61. M. Bonar, *Wayside Wells*, 88.

The more truth we know about the Lord Jesus the more our love will grow.[62]

When the Holy Spirit is filling me with clear and full thoughts of Christ, my whole soul is lifted above sorrow, pressing into the holiest.[63]

You may be asking and not receiving because you have been asking for peace and joy when you should have been asking for Christ.[64]

The man that sees most in the Lord does most for the Lord.[65]

Remembering Christ will take us safely through an evil world into the kingdom of God.[66]

As your head is leaning on His bosom He is moulding you more and more into His likeness.[67]

The Gospel
Whatever a believing man is, he owes it all to the sovereign grace of his God, who made him a vessel of honour; for his "willing and running" (Romans 9:16) come not from himself, but originated with God, 'who sheweth mercy."[68]

---

62. M. Bonar, *Wayside Wells*, 123.
63. M. Bonar, *Wayside Wells*, 174.
64. M. Bonar, *Wayside Wells*, 178–79.
65. M. Bonar, *Wayside Wells*, 188.
66. M. Bonar, *Wayside Wells*, 197.
67. M. Bonar, *Wayside Wells*, 205.
68. A. A. Bonar, *Rev. David Sandeman*, 3.

There is nothing in all the universe which so proclaims God's holy wrath against sin, as that blood of Christ, which is the only meeting-place between an unholy sinner and a holy God.[69]

Our works do not save us, our ill-success will not destroy us, our corruptions and imperfections will only make us more indebted to Jesus forever. He that believeth shall be saved.[70]

"He is All my salvation." Christ is my obedience to the law, my satisfaction for having broken the law, my payment of the ten thousand talents I owe, my righteousness![71]

I notice now that continual omission of the Gospel in our sermons, or passing from it quickly, arises from self-righteousness…self-righteousness is such in ministers and people that nothing but incessant repetition of the Gospel can be right.[72]

Men speak of the dignity of human nature. There is no dignity in a lost sinner. The dignity of human nature is to be reconciled to God.[73]

God pardons according to the greatness of His mercy, not according to the smallness of our sins.[74]

69. A. A. Bonar, *Sheaves*, 99.

70. M. Bonar, *Diary and Life*, 111.

71. M. Bonar, *Diary and Life*, 117.

72. M. Bonar, *Diary and Life*, 161.

73. M. Bonar, *Heavenly Springs*, 71.

74. M. Bonar, *Wayside Wells*, 133.

We are not told that Christ suffered, the just for the unjust, that He might bring us to heaven, but that He might bring us to God.[75]

Salvation is a greater work than creation. There were no obstacles in creation. In salvation there were a thousand. It was not, "He spake and it was done," but "He suffered and died ere it was done."[76]

Redemption implies redemption from the practice of sin, as well as from its guilt.[77]

For there is nothing that Christ the Redeemer has won that He will not share with us.[78]

Holiness
We must give most earnest and continual attention to our personal holiness and growth, even for the sake of winning others.[79]

Led to reflect much upon the fact that our place in Christ's kingdom will be determined by our progress in holiness personally, as much as by the efforts we have used for converting men to Jesus.[80]

Holiness is the great secret of a full way of preaching.[81]

---

75. M. Bonar, *Wayside Wells*, 135.
76. M. Bonar, *Wayside Wells*, 154.
77. M. Bonar, *Wayside Wells*, 167.
78. Ferguson, *Rev. A. A. Bonar*, 279.
79. A. A. Bonar, *Gospel Basics*, 68.
80. M. Bonar, *Diary and Life*, 36.
81. M. Bonar, *Diary and Life*, 38.

Lord, before I finish my course, may I reach further into the mystery of Godliness, and have more power with Thee to bring down blessing on earth.[82]

Holiness of heart and life is what I find I need more than anything, a heart daily filled and burning with fresh views of divine love.[83]

It is a test of our progress in sanctification if we are willing to have our faults pointed out to us, without getting angry.[84]

Purity of heart (Psalm 26:6) depends upon the place we are giving in our conscience to the blood of Christ.[85]

A great feature of holiness is power to bear hard and heavy burdens.[86]

It is not by smiting on your breast that you will grow holy, but by looking on Him who was smitten for you.[87]

It is not ceasing to do evil and learning to do well that sanctifies us. It is breathing the atmosphere of the love of Christ.[88]

I think it is a very poor kind of holiness that does not make us care for others.[89]

---

82. M. Bonar, *Diary and Life*, 221.
83. M. Bonar, *Diary and Life*, 346.
84. M. Bonar, *Diary and Life*, 353.
85. M. Bonar, *Diary and Life*, 393.
86. M. Bonar, *Heavenly Springs*, 39.
87. M. Bonar, *Heavenly Springs*, 71–72.
88. M. Bonar, *Heavenly Springs*, 102.
89. M. Bonar, *Heavenly Springs*, 191.

You are not very holy if you are not very kind.[90]

No one will ever be holy who is not much alone with God.[91]

The holiest believer is he who sees Christ best.[92]

According as God is more and more our portion, so is our progress in holiness.[93]

God alone is sufficient to satisfy the craving of our heart. As we grow in experience of this we grow in holiness.[94]

The reason some of us make slow progress in holiness is that we do not begin by forgetting.[95]

Christ's leaving us nothing to do in justification has left us free to bend all our strength towards sanctification.[96]

There is a special blessing upon those who live separate from the world. The Lord will come near those who are likest to Himself.[97]

The deeper holiness, the less selfishness. The more holiness, the more love.[98]

90. M. Bonar, *Reminiscences*, 125.
91. M. Bonar, *Wayside Wells*, 3.
92. M. Bonar, *Wayside Wells*, 34.
93. M. Bonar, *Wayside Wells*, 73.
94. M. Bonar, *Wayside Wells*, 74.
95. M. Bonar, *Wayside Wells*, 138.
96. M. Bonar, *Wayside Wells*, 167.
97. M. Bonar, *Wayside Wells*, 167.
98. M. Bonar, *Wayside Wells*, 193.

Real holiness is entirely free from selfishness, and real holiness is so tender that it can yearn over misery in a way peculiarly its own.[99]

The Holy Spirit

There is awe upon the spirit of the man whom the Spirit fills, and deepest reverence; for he feels Jehovah's presence with him.[100]

Our only hope is in the Holy Spirit. Eloquence will not move a man's conscience, nor will intellectual power. It is the Spirit that we need, the outpouring of the Holy Spirit.[101]

The kind, patient, longsuffering love of the Spirit is infinitely wonderful. He works calmly, and (we may say) in self-hiding silence, willing to be unnoticed in His working.[102]

Unless I go forth among them, filled with the Holy Spirit, I see that all will be in vain.[103]

If we are filled with the Spirit, God will bless everything about us, the tones of our voice, even the putting out of our hand.[104]

Felt after speaking today how much may be effected by

99. M. Bonar, *Wayside Wells*, 195.
100. A. A. Bonar, *Sheaves*, 35.
101. A. A. Bonar, *Sheaves*, 39.
102. A. A. Bonar, *Sheaves*, 63–64.
103. M. Bonar, *Diary and Life*, 131.
104. M. Bonar, *Diary and Life*, 134.

a very few words when a person is filled with the Holy Ghost. We can afford to be short.[105]

There is more originality in a full heart than in anything else.[106]

The fulness of the Spirit does not manifest itself in mere feeling. It always shows itself in some grace.[107]

If we are believers we have the Holy Spirit dwelling in us, but that is quite a different thing from having the Holy Spirit working in us, and manifesting Himself.[108]

Men of common gifts may have great power, if filled with the Holy Spirit.[109]

It is Thou, Holy Spirit, Who dost gently lead every soul to Christ, and put the sinner's hand into the hand of Christ.[110]

The Spirit does not lead a sinner to Christ, and take farewell of him. He abides with him. No sooner has the blood cleansed the chamber than the Holy Spirit is there, and makes it a temple.[111]

To look on the Son is the Father's heaven. To show Him to us is the Holy Spirit's heaven.[112]

---

105. M. Bonar, *Diary and Life*, 190.
106. M. Bonar, *Diary and Life*, 321.
107. M. Bonar, *Heavenly Springs*, 24.
108. M. Bonar, *Wayside Wells*, 7.
109. M. Bonar, *Wayside Wells*, 103.
110. M. Bonar, *Wayside Wells*, 105.
111. M. Bonar, *Wayside Wells*, 107–8.
112. M. Bonar, *Wayside Wells*, 108.

The Holy Spirit makes us ingenious in doing good. Never say, "I cannot find a sphere of labour." A believer filled with the Spirit finds out what to do.[113]

Humility

Of all ways the most thorough, to make a man humble and self-abased, is for him to see in the light of Christ what he is in himself.[114]

There are two great lessons to me at the present: willing to be nothing, if God so please, and prayer for the past opportunities being blessed.[115]

This morning, after much prayer, I was led to see that my present unhappiness rose from my unwillingness to be humbled and be nothing. I desire now just to enjoy Christ as my Lord and my Friend, and let him send me among men, or keep me unknown and unoccupied as he pleases.[116]

Lord, enable me to live under the smile of Thy love, willing not to be noticed upon earth, if so I may glorify Thee more.[117]

The soul of a "weaned child" is what I seek: meek and lowly in heart, with the eye upon the Lord alone. In this there is rest to the soul.[118]

---

113. M. Bonar, *Wayside Wells*, 150.
114. A. A. Bonar, *Gospel Basics*, 132.
115. M. Bonar, *Diary and Life*, 35.
116. M. Bonar, *Diary and Life*, 35.
117. M. Bonar, *Diary and Life*, 102.
118. M. Bonar, *Diary and Life*, 139.

Yet envy is my hurt, and today I have been seeking grace to rejoice exceedingly over the usefulness of others, even where it casts me into the shade.[119]

Felt today that what I must be is simply this, a channel down which the water is to run.[120]

All I can do for rest and peace is to hide myself from myself in the merit of my Lord. The shadow of the Great Rock is over me.[121]

I see the only life worth living is to live for others.[122]

That God has used me is nothing else than the merest sovereign grace.[123]

Startled while reading Luke 13:30 [And indeed there are last who will be first, and there are first who will be last]. It seems to warn some of us older ministers that it may be we may become self-confident, thinking that because of the past time we must of course stand out still superior to others.[124]

Have been more and more led to be unwilling to speak of work done by myself or my congregation. It is so difficult to escape from self-importance.[125]

119. M. Bonar, *Diary and Life*, 145.
120. M. Bonar, *Diary and Life*, 147.
121. M. Bonar, *Diary and Life*, 200.
122. M. Bonar, *Diary and Life*, 203.
123. M. Bonar, *Diary and Life*, 247.
124. M. Bonar, *Diary and Life*, 252.
125. M. Bonar, *Diary and Life*, 253.

The poorer the materials, just the more thereby will He display His "wisdom" in forming out of me a wonderful vessel of glory![126]

The best part of all Christian work is that part which only God sees. Service for the Master that everybody praises is very dangerous service.[127]

Do much, and say little about it, and think not about what brethren say of you.[128]

It is not a sight of our sinful heart that humbles us, it is a sight of Jesus Christ: I am undone *because mine eyes have seen the King*.[129]

You need not be afraid of too much grace. Great grace never makes a man proud.[130]

I am not, and never was, a great or popular preacher. I have been only an earnest expounder of God's Word, longing to save sinners and edify the saved.[131]

The way to rise high in Christ's kingdom is to serve much.[132]

Self-forgetting work is heavenly work.[133]

126. M. Bonar, *Diary and Life*, 263.
127. M. Bonar, *Diary and Life*, 322.
128. M. Bonar, *Diary and Life*, 337.
129. M. Bonar, *Diary and Life*, 393.
130. M. Bonar, *Diary and Life*, 394.
131. M. Bonar, *Diary and Life*, 405.
132. M. Bonar, *Heavenly Springs*, 50.
133. M. Bonar, *Heavenly Springs*, 51.

It takes us all our days to learn these two things—to be meek and lowly.[134]

Pride is one of the weeds that spring up most readily in our hearts. If allowed, it would grow till it covered the Cross itself.[135]

If you have got such a sight of yourself as makes you lie very low, then, when emptied of self, there is room for Him to fill you with His presence.[136]

Joy

What are some of the elements of heaven? Surely one is joy—holy joy, joy in the Lord. Now, nothing sanctifies more than this joy.[137]

Also I have been taught that joy in the Spirit is the frame in which God blesses us to others. Joy arises from fellowship with Him.[138]

There is an intense joy in God which I have not yet drawn out of Him.[139]

The more I have been able to make God my chief joy the less do I feel in any way tormented with earthly desires, and I see myself surrounded with comforts.[140]

---

134. M. Bonar, *Heavenly Springs*, 130.
135. M. Bonar, *Wayside Wells*, 127.
136. M. Bonar, *Wayside Wells*, 163.
137. A. A. Bonar, *Sheaves*, 18.
138. M. Bonar, *Diary and Life*, 86.
139. M. Bonar, *Diary and Life*, 91.
140. M. Bonar, *Diary and Life*, 99.

Now remember, whenever I see you looking sad or down-cast, I will ask you when you cut the Book of Psalms out of the Bible![141]

The oil of joy calms down the waves of trouble.[142]

A gloomy believer is surely an anomaly in Christ's kingdom.[143]

"Rejoice!" is as much a command as "Repent!"[144]

Cultivate joy as much as you cultivate honesty and uprightness.[145]

"The joy of the Lord is your strength." Whatever is burdening you, get back to the joy of the Lord, and you are above the trouble.[146]

There are far more people made to think by seeing the joy of believers, and their satisfaction in Christ, than by any word they speak.[147]

Do not refuse joy from the Man of Sorrows, for He gained it by His suffering.[148]

Gospel joy never evaporates in telling.[149]

141. M. Bonar, *Diary and Life*, 348.
142. M. Bonar, *Diary and Life*, 387.
143. M. Bonar, *Diary and Life*, 388.
144. M. Bonar, *Heavenly Springs*, 59.
145. M. Bonar, *Heavenly Springs*, 59.
146. M. Bonar, *Heavenly Springs*, 119.
147. M. Bonar, *Reminiscences*, 270.
148. M. Bonar, *Wayside Wells*, 97.
149. M. Bonar, *Wayside Wells*, 98.

True godliness is just joy in God.[150]

There is much holy strength in joy.[151]

Joy does not depend upon our having or wanting earthly things; it depends upon our fellowship with God.[152]

Love
It is just the infinite strength of this Love—Love that will never unloose its grasp which keeps a believer, in spite of earth and hell and his own corruption.[153]

There is no love so mighty as the Spirit's love—no love which will bear so much with us except the love of the Father and of the Son.[154]

The heat of love, not the fire of wrath, is to melt our souls and pour forth our feelings.[155]

I want to live in the love of God, for God, enjoying God, glorifying God, and every day able to tell what new discovery I have made in the fulness of Christ.[156]

As we get into the enjoyment of Thy love may we find that we need scarcely any other heaven either here or

---

150. M. Bonar, *Wayside Wells*, 99.
151. M. Bonar, *Wayside Wells*, 99.
152. M. Bonar, *Wayside Wells*, 100.
153. A. A. Bonar, *Gospel Basics*, 25.
154. A. A. Bonar, *Gospel Basics*, 29.
155. A. A. Bonar, *Leviticus*, 56.
156. M. Bonar, *Diary and Life*, 150.

hereafter—only more of that love and the continuance of it.[157]

Love is the *motive* for working, joy is the *strength* for working.[158]

If we would learn holy love to others, let us learn it from Christ's holy love to us.[159]

God's love to us is unchanging, unceasing, indescribably unselfish.[160]

"Keep yourselves in the love of God!" Never lose the sight and sense of God's love to you.[161]

Do not test your love by emotion, but by obedience.[162]

Prayer
O, may the spirit of prayer be given me every day, and the gifts of the Spirit.[163]

This shows me a lesson, that I must pray as much as if I were nothing, and labour as much as if I were to do all.[164]

God has this week been impressing much upon me the

157. M. Bonar, *Diary and Life*, 335.
158. M. Bonar, *Diary and Life*, 348.
159. M. Bonar, *Wayside Wells*, 185.
160. M. Bonar, *Wayside Wells*, 186.
161. M. Bonar, *Wayside Wells*, 187.
162. M. Bonar, *Wayside Wells*, 187.
163. M. Bonar, *Diary and Life*, 21.
164. M. Bonar, *Diary and Life*, 24.

way of redeeming time for prayer by learning to pray while walking or going from place to place.[165]

Today I am setting my face to fast and pray for enlightenment and refreshing. Until I can get up to the measure of at least two hours in *pure prayer* every day, I shall not be contented. Meditation and reading besides.[166]

I feel that, unless the soul be saturated with prayer and faith, little good may be expected from preaching.[167]

I see that fasting and retirement, along with prayer, should go together.[168]

What is real prayer but a letter to the Lord Jesus, reminding Him of His words and of our needs?[169]

My chief desire should be on this day to be a man of prayer, for there is not want of speaking and writing and preaching and teaching and warning; but there *is* a need of the Holy Spirit to make all this effectual.[170]

Fully convinced by Scripture and past experience especially, and by the experience of all saints, that the best thing I can do, in my study and mode of conducting work, will be to give more time to prayer, and always to give it the earliest place in my employments.[171]

165. M. Bonar, *Diary and Life*, 60.
166. M. Bonar, *Diary and Life*, 63.
167. M. Bonar, *Diary and Life*, 67.
168. M. Bonar, *Diary and Life*, 73.
169. M. Bonar, *Diary and Life*, 93.
170. M. Bonar, *Diary and Life*, 102.
171. M. Bonar, *Diary and Life*, 106.

I have prospered, as to getting sermons and help in them, ever since I made it a rule not to fix thought upon a subject till I had prayed somewhat fully for particular help as to the subject, doctrine, illustration, and application.[172]

Prayer, prayer, prayer must be more a business than it has been.[173]

I see that unless I keep up short prayer every day throughout the day, at intervals, I lose the spirit of prayer. I would never lose sight any hour of the Lamb in the midst of the throne, and if I have this sight I shall be able to pray.[174]

Lord, it is still prayer, prayer, prayer that I am deficient in.[175]

Paul found time, in the midst of a thousandfold more to occupy him, to pray for individual cases often and much. Prayer should make time for itself.[176]

More and more do I learn that continual watchfulness unto prayer is essential to right preaching, right visiting, right conversation, right reading of the Word.[177]

Pray much, and you will be very near the King, for He has a special love to petitions.[178]

Thanksgiving is the very air of heaven.[179]

---

172. M. Bonar, *Diary and Life*, 113.
173. M. Bonar, *Diary and Life*, 115.
174. M. Bonar, *Diary and Life*, 152.
175. M. Bonar, *Diary and Life*, 155.
176. M. Bonar, *Diary and Life*, 196.
177. M. Bonar, *Diary and Life*, 210.
178. M. Bonar, *Diary and Life*, 337.
179. M. Bonar, *Diary and Life*, 387.

Prayer is seed sown on the heart of God.[180]

Fasting is abstaining from all that interferes with prayer.[181]

I sin against the Lord by labouring more than I pray.[182]

Incessant work seems to me to be more than ever a snare, hindering prayer in several ways.[183]

Always follow your work with believing prayer.[184]

If we prayed more we should not have to work so hard.[185]

There are some blessings which are only to be got by importunity.[186]

"All things are naked and opened unto the eyes of Him with Whom we have to do." Let us, therefore, come boldly, for He Who knows the very worst about us gives the invitation.[187]

Take care of expecting an indefinite answer. That is the danger of an indefinite prayer.[188]

The prayer of one has often prevailed for millions.[189]

180. M. Bonar, *Heavenly Springs*, 14.
181. M. Bonar, *Heavenly Springs*, 15.
182. M. Bonar, *Heavenly Springs*, 106.
183. M. Bonar, *Heavenly Springs*, 106.
184. M. Bonar, *Heavenly Springs*, 107.
185. M. Bonar, *Wayside Wells*, 65.
186. M. Bonar, *Wayside Wells*, 67.
187. M. Bonar, *Wayside Wells*, 110.
188. M. Bonar, *Wayside Wells*, 111.
189. M. Bonar, *Wayside Wells*, 190.

Revival

We must continue in prayer if we are to get an outpouring of the Spirit.[190]

Revivals begin with God's own people; the Holy Spirit touches their heart anew, and gives them new fervour and compassion, and zeal, new light and life, and when He has thus come to you, He next goes forth to the valley of dry bones.[191]

I must, through grace, never more let a day pass in which I have not called on the Lord to pour out His Spirit upon us, and upon the nations abroad, wherever the Gospel is preached.[192]

Scripture

I find that reading much Scripture beforehand is excellent preparation for prayer.[193]

In my ordinary reading of Scripture, I often get a single expression which serves as a key-note to my prayers, and sets my soul in order.[194]

Prayer will be very lame and dry if it does not come from reading the Scriptures.[195]

---

190. A. A. Bonar, *Sheaves*, 39.
191. A. A. Bonar, *Sheaves*, 77.
192. M. Bonar, *Diary and Life*, 282.
193. M. Bonar, *Diary and Life*, 61.
194. M. Bonar, *Diary and Life*, 203.
195. M. Bonar, *Diary and Life*, 334.

Every line in this inspired Bible is wet with the dew of the Spirit's love.[196]

Make Thy Word a candle to reveal sin, and a leaf from the tree of life to heal.[197]

Faith gets no nourishment but by the study of the Word. Feelings do not nourish faith.[198]

The Second Coming of Christ

The contemplation of Christ's Second Coming does thus help us to fix upon the very marrow of his First Coming.[199]

No Christian denies the fact of the Second Coming of Christ. But very many, even the most godly in later days, have failed to meditate much upon this blessed hope.[200]

The root of the neglect lies here; men have not felt the joy and the holy influences which the Second Coming yields.[201]

This unceasing regard to the Lord's Coming is surely one scriptural ingredient in all real holiness.[202]

O, my friends, your faith is incomplete if you do not live in the daily faith of a coming Saviour.[203]

---

196. M. Bonar, *Diary and Life*, 397.
197. M. Bonar, *Wayside Wells*, 33.
198. M. Bonar, *Wayside Wells*, 34.
199. A. A. Bonar, *Redemption*, 10.
200. A. A. Bonar, *Redemption*, 33.
201. A. A. Bonar, *Redemption*, 34.
202. A. A. Bonar, *Redemption*, 37.
203. A. A. Bonar, *Redemption*, 162.

We do not say that *the details* of the Second Coming must thus deeply affect us; what we say is, that *the event* must, or rather, that *He who is to come* must be so expected and longed for as to affect us powerfully.[204]

Those saints who feel most keenly the world's enmity, and the Church's imperfection, are those who will most fervently love their Lord's appearing.[205]

The cherishing of this blessed hope, instead of hindering our work, has all along kept us at work, caring comparatively little for the politics of earth. It has been like oil on the wheels, making us seek to abound in the work of the Lord.[206]

I find the thought of Christ's Coming very helpful in keeping me awake. Those who are waiting for His appearing will get a special blessing.[207]

Think of Christ's coming again. This is what sanctifies, what strengthens, what gladdens.[208]

We are to live for the Lord today, and look for His coming tomorrow.[209]

The love that brought Him down once will bring Him back to us a second time.[210]

204. A. A. Bonar, *Redemption*, 352.
205. A. A. Bonar, *Rutherford*, 30.
206. A. A. Bonar, *Sheaves*, 44–45.
207. M. Bonar, *Diary and Life*, 403.
208. M. Bonar, *Heavenly Springs*, 32.
209. M. Bonar, *Heavenly Springs*, 151.
210. M. Bonar, *Wayside Wells*, 117.

The fact that the apostles did not understand our Lord's plain statements about His death might suggest to some of us, What if we, in like manner, be found not understanding plain statements about His coming again?[211]

If our body will be so changed at the resurrection, what our soul will be passes understanding.[212]

Spiritual Growth

Giving well is as needful to our soul's prosperity as doing well, as surely as "the doer of the work is blessed in his deed" (James 1:25), so surely is the willing giver of his substance blessed in his giving.[213]

A true disciple is always learning. Every believer we meet with has something for us if we could only get it.[214]

We are all alike cleansed by the same atoning blood, we all have the same precious faith, but some go further on than others, and get nearer God.[215]

See that your last days are your best days.[216]

Ask any gardener, and he will tell you it is a sad indication of any plant to stop growing.[217]

---

211. M. Bonar, *Wayside Wells*, 118–19.
212. M. Bonar, *Wayside Wells*, 119.
213. A. A. Bonar, *Gospel Basics*, 144.
214. M. Bonar, *Diary and Life*, 327.
215. M. Bonar, *Heavenly Springs*, 115.
216. M. Bonar, *Heavenly Springs*, 159.
217. M. Bonar, *Heavenly Springs*, 160.

It is expected of God's children that they make progress. They are to be always adding to their faith.[218]

The more believers grow, the more hope for those around them.[219]

A special cause of our little growth in grace is our doing nothing for others.[220]

Suffering/Trials

Many solemn sad feelings about my loneliness now, but the Lord can enable me to bear the loss of my beloved wife so as to be more than conqueror. Every man has his burden from the Lord, and glorifies God in proportion as he bears it in the Lord's strength.[221]

The Lord delights to give thee all that is really good, and therefore be assured that in all He takes from thee He meant thee only good and nothing else.[222]

I have learned, in some measure, that the Lord can fill the soul with *Himself*, when He takes away what seemed indispensable to our happiness on earth.[223]

The Fountain of living water feels most satisfying when other waters fail.[224]

218. M. Bonar, *Wayside Wells*, 138.
219. M. Bonar, *Wayside Wells*, 139.
220. M. Bonar, *Wayside Wells*, 184.
221. M. Bonar, *Diary and Life*, 185.
222. M. Bonar, *Diary and Life*, 201.
223. M. Bonar, *Diary and Life*, 258.
224. M. Bonar, *Diary and Life*, 259.

Many things have made earth to me more than ever a wilderness or a land of broken cisterns. But the Lord Jesus is more than ever a full heaven to me.[225]

If we cannot say like Paul "this light affliction," let us at any rate try to say, "It is but for a moment."[226]

We have got more from Paul's prison-house than from his visit to the third heavens.[227]

I find that the more of Christ we enjoy, the more we are able to bear.[228]

Burdens are part of a believer's education.[229]

May those on whom a dark cloud is resting find that it hides the world from them, and makes Christ's presence very sweetly felt.[230]

If you have a dread of any trouble coming, sing, instead of brooding over it.[231]

All testing in the way of trial to God's people is just to separate the sin that He hates from the soul that He loves.[232]

225. M. Bonar, *Diary and Life*, 262.
226. M. Bonar, *Diary and Life*, 350.
227. M. Bonar, *Diary and Life*, 350.
228. M. Bonar, *Diary and Life*, 388.
229. M. Bonar, *Heavenly Springs*, 39.
230. M. Bonar, *Wayside Wells*, 21.
231. M. Bonar, *Wayside Wells*, 23.
232. M. Bonar, *Wayside Wells*, 83.

Suffering is the rude vessel in which He carries to us the water of life.[233]

You can walk through the furnace, for there is one with you who is the Son of God.[234]

---

233. M. Bonar, *Wayside Wells*, 83.
234. Ferguson, *Rev. A. A. Bonar*, 277.

Bonar Collection Tract Titles

Blue Notebook

Notes of an Address Delivered at the Glasgow Fellowship Meeting, 1875

The First of the First-Fruits

Death or Life This Year

The True Heaven, and the Way to It

The Family, a Reflection of Heaven

Behold the Lamb of God! An Address to the Young

The Twelve Stones of Gilgal

Treasured Words

From Strength to Strength: Four Addresses to Young Believers

Brown Notebook

The Books of the Old Testament: Being Brief Notes on the Contents of Each Book, Especially Intended for the Young

Emilia Geddie, a Child of the Covenant Who Died in 1681: An Example Alike to Young and Old

The Manslayers Flight

Some Good Thing; or, The Prince Who Died in Tirzah

The Hiding Place

The Monk of Inchcolm: An Example of Faith for the Year 1869

Gamaliel: A Word to Young Men

Story of Andrew Lindsay

Joy in Christ: The Story of a Young Believer

The Hermit of Sinai: A Narrative from Church History in the Fifth Century

The Martyrs by the Sea: The Story of the Wigtown Sufferers

That Sight

The Children's Missionary Record of the Free Church of Scotland

Bibliography

Bonar, Andrew A. *The Brook Besor*. New York: Robert Carter and Brothers, 1880.

———. *Christ and His Church in the Book of Psalms*. Stoke-on-Trent: Tentmaker Publications, 2012.

———. *A Commentary on Leviticus*. 1966. Reprint, Edinburgh: Banner of Truth, 1998.

———. *The Development of Antichrist*. Essex: Sovereign Grace Advent Testimony, n.d.

———. *From Strength to Strength*. London: Morgan & Scott, n.d.

———. *Gospel Basics*. Edinburgh: Banner of Truth, 2011.

———. *The Gospel Pointing to the Person of Christ*. Edinburgh: Andrew Stevenson, 1888.

———. *Memoir and Remains of Robert Murray M'Cheyne*. Edinburgh: Banner of Truth, 2004.

———. *Memoir of the Life and Brief Ministry of the Rev. David Sandeman, Missionary to China*. London: James Nisbet & Co., 1862. Reprint, Ithaca, N.Y.: Cornell University Press, 1997.

———. *Outlines of Sermons to Children*. Clerical Library. New York: A. C. Armstrong & Son, 1880.

———. *Palestine for the Young*. London: Religious Tract Society, n.d.

———. *Redemption Drawing Nigh*. London: J. Nisbet & Co., 1847.

———. *Sheaves after Harvest*. London: Pickering and Inglis, n.d.

———. *Uncle John Vassar: or, The Fight of Faith*. Preface by Andrew Bonar. Charleston, S.C.: BiblioLife, n.d.

———. Untitled collection of author's tracts and personal notes, bound in two volumes (cited as *Bonar Collection*), privately owned. Publication of cited tracts by Glasgow: Charles Glass & Co., n.d., ca. 1870–1885.

———. *The Visitor's Book of Texts*. Edinburgh: Banner of Truth, 2010.

Bonar, Andrew A., ed. *Letters of Samuel Rutherford*. 1984. Reprint, Edinburgh: Banner of Truth, 2006.

———. *The Old Gospel Way*. Glasgow: Free Presbyterian Church of Scotland, 2016.

Bonar, Andrew, and Robert M. M'Cheyne. *Mission of Discovery* (originally published as *Narrative of a Mission of Inquiry to the Jews from the Church of Scotland in 1839*). Geanies House: Christian Focus Publications, 1996.

Bonar, Marjory. *The Good Pastor*. Belfast: Ambassador Publications, 1999.

Bonar, Marjory, ed. *The Diary and Life of Andrew A. Bonar*. Edinburgh: Banner of Truth, 2013.

———. *Heavenly Springs*. Edinburgh: Banner of Truth, 1986.

———. *Reminiscences of Andrew A. Bonar D. D.* London: Hodder and Stoughton, 1897.

———. *Wayside Wells.* London: Hodder and Stoughton, 1908.

Chalmers, Thomas. *The Expulsive Power of a New Affection.* Minneapolis, Minn.: Curiosmith, 2012.

Dallimore, Arnold. *Forerunner of the Charismatic Movement: The Life of Edward Irving.* Chicago: Moody Bible Institute, 1983.

Dorsett, Lyle. *A Passion for Souls: The Life of D. L. Moody.* Chicago: Moody Publishers, 1997.

Ferguson, Fergus. *Rev. A. A. Bonar. D. D.* Glasgow: John J. Rae, 1893.

Haykin, Michael A. G., and Darrin R. Booker, eds. *Christ Is All: The Piety of Horatius Bonar.* Grand Rapids, Mich.: Reformation Heritage Books, 2007.

Murray, Iain H. "Andrew Bonar and Fellowship with Christ." *The Banner of Truth Magazine* 567, December 2010.

———. *A Scottish Christian Heritage.* Edinburgh: Banner of Truth, 2006.

———. *Seven Leaders.* Edinburgh: Banner of Truth, 2017.

Robertson, Nicoll. *Princes of the Church.* London: Hodder and Stoughton, 1921.

Tyler, Bennet, and Andrew A. Bonar. *Nettleton and His Labors.* Edinburgh: Banner of Truth, 1996.